be seeking, *The World At My Feet* is a great study in the mindset and perseverance required to make things happen. IT'S A GREAT 'ANY-THING'S POSSIBLE' STORY."

**—Mark Crowley, Host, *The Success Radio Show***

"FASCINATING! The first person and candid account of one of America's pioneering women aviators, from her days as a helicopter pilot to her present-day role as a captain of a commercial airliner. THIS BOOK GIVES READERS AN INSIDE ACCOUNT OF WHAT IT TAKES TO BE AMONG THE FIRST AND THE BEST. The amazing, daring accounts of pilot training, and the prejudices battled during her rise through the ranks are revealed in heartfelt, shocking and often times hilarious detail. NO OTHER BOOK ABOUT WOMEN PILOTS HAS DELVED INTO THE SUBJECT OF A WOMAN FLYER WITH SUCH VIGOR. YOU'LL HEAD FOR THE NEAREST FLIGHT SCHOOL!"

**—Peter Heymann, author of**
***When Women Helped Save the World***

"Captain Meryl Getline made her adventurous ascension to Airline Pilothood simply because...she's Meryl! This wonderful memoir has a terrific moral for us all: How by following your own personal, internal compass and staying the course, you can achieve great accomplishments. This book is a whole lotta fun—and inspirational to boot."

**—Jo Myers, KOSI Morning show, Denver**

AN AMAZING AND WONDERFUL MEMOIR BY TOP-NOTCH PILOT MERYL GETLINE of her first 50 years living life to the max—I can't wait to read the sequel!

**—Bonnie Tiburzi, first woman pilot ever to be hired by a**
**major air carrier (American Airlines, 1973)**

How fun to be able to peer into this window of Captain Meryl Getline's adventurous life. ENGAGING. EXCITING. HUMOROUS. COURAGEOUS. UNBELIEVABLE AT TIMES. But real and incredible. Just like Meryl herself."

**—Karen Wira, Wira Associates**

"This is a wonderful memoir, full of interesting stories and events of the author's passage from childhood to becoming an airline Captain. She tells it well, often with humor, but it is also a lesson for all of us on tenacity and how to make a dream come true by will and courage. THIS ISN'T JUST ANOTHER FLYING BOOK, BUT RATHER ONE THAT WILL FIT ON THE BOOKSHELF OF AVIATION HISTORY AND ADVENTURE."
—**Bob Buck, Former Chief Pilot, TWA (Ret.), author of**
*Weather Flying, North Star Over My Shoulder,* **and others**

"GETLINE'S PLUCKY RESOLVE, INGENUITY, PERSIST-ENCE, AND RESOURCEFULNESS CALLS TO MIND WINSTON CHURCHILL: NEVER, NEVER, NEVER, NEVER GIVE UP. It is remarkable how many times she turns 'no' into 'yes' by going around or though obstacles."
—**Paul Brown, President, Airport Concessions, Inc.**
**United Airlines Premier Member**
**Alaska Airlines MVP Gold Member**
**America West Silver Flight Fund Member**

"A unique and inspiring book about so much more than aviation. Captivating, moving and just 'plane' funny! A great book to read again and again when faced with what seem like insurmountable odds. Meryl demonstrates the very meaning of tenacity."
—**Captain Al Carmickle, United Airlines (Ret.)**

"*The World at My Feet* is a heartwarming story of pursuing the American dream. Despite the overwhelming odds stacked against her, Ms. Getline achieved her lifelong goal of being a commercial airline pilot. Her story is an inspiration to women everywhere and anyone who has faced unfair discrimination. This book is for anyone who's been told 'that's not possible' and won't accept 'no' for an answer."
—**David Grossman, freelance travel writer**
**whose work has appeared in USATODAY.com**

MORE PRAISE FOR *THE WORLD AT MY FEET*

"ENGAGING, FUNNY, EDUCATIONAL AND INSPIRA-
TIONAL! Meryl's book makes a great gift for young girls,
teens—even college-age gals (and guys, too!). I can't imagine
any better motivational tool to help shape their futures and career
choices."

**—Captain Mimi Tompkins**
**First Female Pilot for Aloha Airlines**

"An inspirational book for all of us, young and old. Meryl overcame
all the societal, physical, mental, and psychological challenges
thrown at her to achieve a childhood dream. *The World At My Feet*
BELONGS ON EVERYONE'S BOOKSHELF."

**—Herb Shaindlin, *ABC-TV News* Commentator**

"*The World At My Feet* DESERVES TO BE CATEGORIZED AS
AN AVIATION CLASSIC."

**—Robert J. Serling, NY Times best-selling author of**
**The President's Plane Is Missing, The Left Seat, and others**

"I LOVED YOUR BOOK—A FAST READ, VERY ENTER-
TAINING AND A WHOLE LOT OF FUN. The three principles
that have guided Meryl (and me, for that matter) are: 1) never
accept the word 'NO;' 2) the belief that you can be whoever you
want to be; and 3) the belief that nothing is impossible. BRAVO,
MERYL!"

**—Frank W. Abagnale, NY Times best-selling author of**
**(and the basis for the OSCAR-winning motion picture)**
***CATCH ME IF YOU CAN***

"SHE'S GOT 'THE RIGHT STUFF!' A gorgeous book—and a
gorgeous author—that's almost impossible to put down!"

**—Pat Moffett, author of *Fortunate Soldier***

"INSPIRING AND FUN! The story of how a smart, capable, determined woman can best one of the last bastions of male arrogance—the airline cockpit—is a must-read, especially for any airline passenger who ever had even a momentary worry about 'girls' in the commercial cockpit. All my career IT'S BEEN MY PRIVILEGE TO FLY WITH THE FEMALE PIONEERS OF AIRLINE COCKPITS, AND MERYL GETLINE IS A WORTHY REPRESENTATIVE OF THIS RARE AND WONDERFUL BREED OF PROFESSIONAL AERONAUTS."

—**John J. Nance, NY Times best-selling author of** *Pandora's Clock*, *Fire Flight*, **and others**

"Getline is passionately in love with flying . . . PASSENGERS HAVE BEEN KNOWN TO GATHER AROUND HER AT THE END OF A FLIGHT AS IF THEY WERE WAITING TO MEET A CELEBRITY."

—*DENVER POST*

"A BEAUTIFULLY WRITTEN, VERY FUNNY, THOROUGHLY ENGAGING ACCOUNT OF A REMARKABLE PILOT (AND RACONTEUR). Step into the copilot's seat and have the ride of your life with one of America's top commercial pilots."

—**Capt. Edward M. Brittingham, USN (Ret.),** **author of** *Operation Poppy* **and** *SUB CHASER*

"An inspiring read that makes the spirit soar. I loved the book. It also has the added bonus of a Q/A on flying in the back of THE BOOK THAT WILL KEEP THE CONVERSATION GOING (AND ALL THE CURIOUS SATISFIED) ON ANY FLIGHT!"

—**Durward Lewis,** *BD King Press*

"After growing up in a United Airlines family and being a pilot myself, I most enjoyed *The World At My Feet*. Meryl's humorous, irreverent, and even serious-when-needed look at the development of her career as an airline pilot is an easy, enjoyable read. She certainly captures the essence of HER JOURNEY TO BREAK THROUGH THE 'GLASS COCKPIT.' No matter what career an individual may

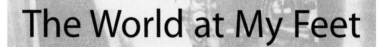

# The World at My Feet

## The True (and Sometimes Hilarious) Adventures of a Lady Airline Captain

### Captain Meryl Getline

Lorrie Press
www.fromthecockpit.com

For more information about this title, please contact:
Lorrie Press
c/o Meryl Getline
1253 Santa Fe Trail
Elizabeth, CO 80107 or
info@fromthecockpit.com

Book design by:
The Floating Gallery
244 Madison Ave, #254
New York, NY 10016
877-822-2500
www.thefloatinggallery.com

Printed in Canada

Meryl Getline
The World At My Feet
1. Author   2. Title
Library of Congress Control Number: 2004104805
ISBN: 0-9754367-0-8

To Order Additional Copies of *The World At My Feet*
call 1-800-345-6665 or log onto www.fromthecockpit.com
and click on "The Book!"

## Acknowledgments

My parents, for allowing my "free-spirit" lifestyle, without which there would have been no book, and for not putting me up for adoption once they found out what an enormous amount of trouble I would be as their daughter. My thanks to them as well for their valuable editorial contributions.

Captain Al Carmickle, United Airlines, Retired, for his technical assistance and immense personal support.

Lorin Getline, my brother, for supplying research materials, for his many editorial contributions and for providing the extra encouragement I needed to get the job done.

Dan Alderman, my dear friend who provided inspiration and encouragement every step of the way.

Karen Wira, for her constant support as a friend and for her many editorial contributions.

Larry Leichman, The Floating Gallery, for his marketing expertise.

Joel Hochman, The Floating Gallery for his technical expertise.

Mia Claudia Wood, for her endless patience in reading, editing and proofing, and for her constant encouragement.

Peter Bartzcak for his cover artwork.

United Airlines First Officer John Fry, for encouraging me to help motivate others with my life story.

To Bette and Gordon Getline, my Mom and Dad, for giving me the freedom to be me.

# CONTENTS

# FOREWORD

The book you're about to read recounts the trials, tribulations, and triumphs of a woman airline pilot. It is not the first work on the subject, but it's the best I've ever read—fair, funny, and inspiring to any girl harboring the same dreams that Meryl Getline made come true.

It also will be reassuring to any airline passenger who might develop a sudden case of white knuckles when a female voice on the cabin PA announces: "This is your captain speaking." I have no doubt such fears were not unusual when women airline pilots were about as numerous as surviving dinosaurs. Now there are hundreds of them, many wearing the coveted four stripes of captain, and the chauvinistic prejudices they once faced have gone into the same limbo as the "Coffee, Tea, or Me?" stigma that once libeled flight attendants.

Meryl Getline was among the first of her sex to crash the barriers of professional discrimination in the airline industry, yet like most of these pioneering pilots hers was a personal crusade, not a desire to become a flying Susan B. Anthony trying to make a point by making loud noises. That was the case also for Emily Howell, the nation's first female airline pilot in modern times who went on to become a Frontier Airlines captain.

It also was true of those who followed her, including Madeline "Mimi" Tompkins. On April 28, 1988, she was the first officer on an Aloha Airlines Boeing 737 that lost 220 feet of the upper fuselage, causing an explosive decompression that injured every passenger and sucked a flight attendant out of the aircraft. Tompkins' professionalism in helping the captain land the crippled airliner safely brought widespread praise and eventually won her upgrading to captain.

Getline is cut out of the same cloth as Howell and Tompkins, yet her story is refreshingly different in many respects, full of as much wry humor as the frustrating barriers she encountered. She obtained her first—and unsuccessful— airline interview because the carrier she had applied to thought "Meryl" was a man's name. But from then on, her experiences as a trainee and eventual promotion into jetliner cockpits is a textbook lesson in perseverance, patience and determination. Her narrative is even more inspirational because her motivation was not resentment against the industry's reluctance to hire women pilots, but was based purely on a love of flying that dated back to childhood.

It is for this thick vein of objectivity that runs through her story that *The World At My Feet* deserves to be categorized as an aviation classic. The bonus is Meryl's sense of humor—her encounter with a Goodyear blimp when she was an air traffic controller is worth the price of the book all by itself. Another bonus, I submit, is that it may reform a few males whose negative views on female competence usually are expressed by bellowing: "Those #$*# women drivers!"

Getline reminds us how far we've come since the days when even the world's most famous woman pilot, Amelia Earhart, was subjected to a patronizing kind of prejudice. In 1929 an airline hired her supposedly to help promote air travel among women—she was given the fancy title of "assistant to the general traffic manager." Her hiring was simply a publicity stunt involving the launching of the carrier's 48-hour air-rail transcontinental service, using an airplane for the daytime legs and trains by night. But she went solely as a passenger, after christening the airplane for photographers, and her employment lasted only until the inaugural trip was completed.

A personal postscript...

Some years ago, the Aviation/Space Writers Association held its annual convention in Atlanta, and I suggested that one of the events should include a news conference featuring women pilots from the airlines and military. I made a point of insisting that they wear their uniforms—I had a hunch this would impress the hell out of any chauvinistic colleagues in attendance. It sure did. They showed up as instructed, and the sighs of admiration would have created a 20-knot headwind on a runway. I remember one of the airline pilots was the daughter of cowboy movie star Clint Walker—she was a copilot with Western Airlines, a tall, beautiful blonde. The Air Force, Navy, Marines, and Coast Guard had provided equally impressive women pilots, and they all fielded questions with polished skill.

After reading her book, I wish we had invited Meryl Getline, too. She would have belonged right up there on that podium.

Robert J. Serling
Former Aviation editor
United Press International

# INTRODUCTION

How many people in life benefit from the crystal clear direction that comes from knowing what they want to do early in life? Do the benefits of self-determinism ever outweigh the benefits of a goal easily attained?

In her work, Getline makes a strong case for having a clearly defined goal in life, through the lens of her own struggle to become one of the first female major commercial airline pilots in the world. She inspires with plucky resolve, ingenuity, and resourcefulness in a way that compares with the struggles of a real-life little engine that could. She provides a living example of the sentiments expressed by Winston Churchill more than 50 years ago: Never, never, never, never give up, no matter how arduous the path or how presumably unattainable the goal. Throughout the story, it becomes progressively more remarkable how many times she turns no into yes by going around or though obstacles. It also becomes progressively clear that she does not heed her detractors, which leads to the mountain of hilarious adventures that no one could ever make up. At one point, the story becomes so amazing that one feels compelled to check the cover of the book to verify what one is reading.

Many useful lessons are displayed in grand fashion, such as the rewards of persistence, of being relentlessly focused on one's goals, and of keeping an open mind. Perhaps the most valuable, however, is that of following the rabbit hole, so to speak, to see where it ends up. Many of the successes and unique experiences shared by Getline in her work result from doggedly following a thread of her dream to be a pilot, sometimes ending up in an entirely different place than she originally expected. For example, while at a regional transport company, her adherence to this principle takes her halfway around the world to Iran in the blink of an eye! This instance also illustrates the very tangible benefit that accrues to she who has the courage and initiative to commit to action before the competition.

This book is moving and funny without being ponderous and high-handed. The style is conversational, as if Getline was seated next to the reader on a two-hour commuter flight, talking about how she got to where she is today. She effectively explains how she overcame obstacles without passing judgment on the obstructers, leaving the reader free to formulate her own opinions about the injustice of prejudice. She also provides key insight into the secretive world of commercial airline pilots, which is a proverbial black box to all but only the most frequent travelers. Because of her indomitable spirit and her capacity to move like a powerful vector towards her goals, without needlessly burdening the reader with self-righteous prattle about the sins of discrimination, this work becomes a demonstrative tale about the struggle against bias and oppression that resonates well with many different kinds of people.

It is apparent that those who got to know Getline along her path to success benefited from knowing a rare and superior person. Those who crave achievement of their goals would do well to follow suit by reading this book.

Paul Brown
President, Airport Concessions, Inc.
United Airlines Premier Member
Alaska Airlines MVP Gold Member
America West Silver Flight Fund Member

## PROLOGUE

Iran, 1979

I dove into the bushes along the beach right behind my friend Toba. "What are we *doing*?" I gasped.

Moments earlier we had been windsurfing on the Caspian Sea in northern Iran—or, more precisely, I'd been falling off the sailboard while trying to learn. Sailboards in the 1970s were kind of big and clunky, and anyway, there wasn't much breeze to get going. Nevertheless, the afternoon was gorgeous, clear and quiet. The sun was bright and the air warm. Perfect for the beach.

About fifty or sixty people were in and about the water. Children played along the shore and in the shallows as watchful mothers chatted away under the weight of their drenched *chadors*, the full-length black robes worn by Muslim women.

I had just fallen off the board yet again when Toba called, her accented English urgent. "We must get out, *right now!*"

"Why?" I was just getting the hang of this windsurfing thing.

I heard her say something in her native language, Farsi, but I couldn't make out what it was. Then she shouted in English, pointing to the shore, "The Beach Police are coming!"

"The what?" I laughed. At first I thought she was kidding, but when I turned to look, it was quite obvious she wasn't. In the distance, two men in drab olive military dress, with full gear, were driving in a camouflaged Jeep toward us. It was clear these guys weren't lifeguards. They were about three miles away, giving us just enough time to get out.

We ditched the sailboard and swam hard for land. The Beach Police were only about a hundred yards away by the time we reached the shore. Our lungs were about to burst. Running hard toward the bushes against the wall that lined the perimeter of the sand, I could hear the shouts of the men hot on our trail. Of all the languages I'd spent my life learning, Farsi wasn't one of them. I made a mental note to change that.

With my eyes on the Beach Police, I raced to the bushes, blindly following Toba as she suddenly dropped to all fours and scuttled through a tiny hole in the wall covered by underbrush. Little branches scraped my knees and hands. I realized she was following a path carved out beneath the bushes, like the ones rabbits and other small creatures make.

After what seemed like an eternity, she stopped in front of a little alcove. Sitting down, she patted the dirt next to her. I sat, too, and then, like prairie dogs, we poked our heads above the bushes in the direction of the beach. The Jeep was still there, and the Beach Police milled about. "Give it a minute or two," she said, reaching into her bikini top. "Besides, I need a smoke."

Wrapped in plastic was a soft pack of cigarettes and book of matches. She pulled them out and lit a cigarette, inhaling deeply. "Oh," she closed her eyes, enjoying the feeling of the smoke in her lungs, "that is good."

"Put that thing out!" I hissed. "They'll see the smoke."

"Not likely," she dismissed me with a wave of her cigarette.

I scrunched up my nose and blew the smoke away from my face, then began to inspect my knees.

"Sorry, Meryl. I didn't mean to put smoke in your face." Then she noticed my scratches. "Those, also. Sorry."

"So, what now?"

"I finish my smoke, we go back."

"Well," I sighed, "okay." Maybe the Beach Police will have moved on for good. Suddenly, I realized I had no idea why we had run in the first place. "What *are* Beach Police?"

She puffed languidly on her cigarette. "The bathing suits. They stop people for dress code infractions. Things like that."

"For wearing bathing suits? They need the military for that?" I was incredulous. "So that's it, I guess. No more windsurfing."

"No, no. It will be fine. You don't want to go put on a *chador*, do you? Just keep an eye out. I will, too. If you see them, if it looks like they see us, we have to run for it."

I rolled my eyes, frustrated. "What happens if they catch us?"

She frowned, and replied vaguely, "Not much."

"And you've been doing this—" I waved my hand around our little hiding space, "—for a while?"

"Mm-hmm," she inhaled.

"Okay, okay. Good. Our chances are pretty good then. You're an expert."

She shrugged.

"With so many countries sharing borders around this water, don't the Iranians have something better to do than chase girls in bikinis?"

She shrugged again, but this time with an entirely different meaning. "Apparently they need something to do. Men, you know."

All I wanted to do was be in the water, left alone to enjoy the day. Somehow, I should have known it couldn't be that simple. Nothing about this trip had been simple from the start.

Toba took another drag off her cigarette and crushed the stub into the dirt. She got up to survey the scene. "I still see them walking the beach, and they are in no hurry." Sitting back down, she reached once more for her pack of cigarettes. "We may be here a while longer than I thought. So tell me," she said, "how did you become a pilot? It is difficult, no, even in America?"

And so, in the bushes along the shore of the Caspian Sea, hiding from the Iranian Beach Police while the sailboard drifted lazily toward Turkmenistan, and the day wore on, I started thinking about how it all began ...

# CHAPTER 1

## I Gotta Fly!

"I have to fly, Dad," I stated matter-of-factly. At eleven-years-old, I had already figured out that I wanted to be on an airplane.

My father, ensconced in his chair, peered at me over the top of his Sunday paper. "How do you expect to do that?"

"You'd better start flapping," Scott, the youngest of my three older brothers, said as he was leaving the room.

Turning away from the unwanted distraction, I put my hands on my hips and waited for my father to tell me no. I already knew that we'd have to go through a series of denials before I got what I wanted.

He looked at me and said, "Sweetheart, you can't fly. You know that."

I stared at the front of his paper, behind which he had just retreated. Scott snickered, and then headed out as I glared after him. How in the world could things so clear to me be beyond everybody else? "In an *airplane*. I have to fly in an airplane. By myself."

That brought the paper down to his lap. "Meryl, wherever did you get that idea?"

Maybe it was because my father was an aerospace engineer and went on frequent business trips that required air travel, or maybe I was simply born with the need to roam and see beyond my own backyard. Whatever the reason, I knew early on I had to travel. I had to fly.

It could have been the time we took my middle brother, Lorin, to the Los Angeles International airport for a chartered flight to Scandinavia. A talented musician, he performed with an orchestra from the Idyllwild School of Music and the Arts located in Idyllwild, California, which had accepted an invitation to play in Europe. There was even a documentary made about the trip called *The Sounds of Sweet Harmony*. Every once in a while, it still surfaces on PBS.

If only I could have packed myself up in one of Lorin's suitcases, I would have gone in a heartbeat. My whole family was thrilled with the news, but his trip utterly and completely captured my imagination. I pretended over and over that *I* was the one going.

Even when I was very little, I had an interest in far off places. From my earliest memories, I was taken with the German language. I liked the way it sounded and would try to imitate it whenever I happened to hear any German on TV. I would watch movies about World War II, as there was invariably dialogue in German with English subtitles. The first book my parents gave me when I started to read was an edition of "Sleeping Beauty" written in English and German, with the German spelled both phonetically and correctly. By the time I was six I would arrive at the dinner table with some phrase to try out on my father, who spoke some German.

Music was another integral part of my upbringing. I was born into a house full of music. There were instruments all over the house, and when someone wasn't playing music, we were listening to records or the radio. All of us kids, Scott, Lorin, Ned, and I, were very much involved in music throughout the years. Once Lorin, a music major in college, came to the high school Scott and I still attended and conducted the orchestra we both played in for a semester.

I can't think of a balalaika without pleasant memories of an unlikely train ride with an especially musical contingent of the Russian Red Army. I can't hear a violin without remembering the incredibly talented gypsies I'd seen in my travels, playing traditional folk songs in Romania and Bulgaria as they rumbled about the countryside in their covered wagons. To this day, music is very much a part of all our lives.

I grew up listening along with my mother to the classical station on the radio in the living room. My dad played piano and my brothers played a variety of instruments. Never one to be out of the picture, I played, too: piano and French horn. Later I played a number of stringed instruments.

Once, during Tchaikovsky's 1812 Overture, one of my favorite records, Scott and I took trashcan lids out of the garage. Every time the cymbals played, we were right there with our aluminum trashcan lids crashing along with them, standing just outside the living room window so our mother could watch. Even my canary, Tweeter, had a penchant for classical music and always sang frantically with the 1812 Overture—loud enough that you could hear him in-between all the racket we were making. Lorin had a less musically inclined parakeet named Woofer. I didn't get the joke for years.

When I was six, my mother took me to a performance of the Polish State Folk Ballet in town after Lorin got sick and couldn't go. She hadn't expected that, at such a young age, I'd be particularly interested. The experience was an epiphany. Not only was I completely mesmerized by the music, I was also fascinated by the fact that, according to the program, the entire ensemble—orchestra, dancers, choreographers, costume-makers—lived in a castle in Poland where they trained for performances throughout the world.

During the intermission, my mother bought me everything they had for sale including a full-color program, biographical material about the troupe, and a record, every word and note of which I memorized. I loved the fact that the words were in a different language. I imitated the sounds and at least imagined I understood some of the words. The songs had an English translation in the program, and I actually was able to make out some of the meaning, but at the time I just wanted to be able to sing along with the record. Thereafter, I was completely enamored of folk music, and my mother started taking me to every folk music concert that came to town. I remember performances by the Russian Balalaika Orchestra, which I was later to see live in Moscow, the Violinists of Romania, The Pipers of the Royal Scottish Fusiliers and many, many more.

Since I also took ballet as a little girl, my mother began taking me to lots of ballets as well. Prokovief's *Romeo and Juliet* made a huge impression on me at a very young age. I think it surprised my mother then, as it surprises me now, that such "heavy" music held such joy for me. I remember seeing the Royal Danish Ballet perform Rossini's *La Boutique Fantasque* ("The Toy Shop"). That's one record I practically wore out before I even started the first grade. I especially loved Baroque music with the trumpets and pipe organs, and learned to play different pieces and instruments by ear and by reading music. If there was music playing, I wanted to join in. I loved Bach, Telemann and Purcell, and wanted to hear every composer there was. Prokovief's *Peter and the Wolf* was, and still is, one of my favorites.

The thought of traveling to a mysterious destination took seed in my imagination the day we took Lorin to the airport, along with the fascination of music and foreign languages. All of this was spinning through my brain as we made our way to see Lorin off to Scandinavia that day at LAX. The airplane was a Scandinavian Airlines System DC-8. It was quite simply the most gorgeous thing I'd ever seen. From the moment I saw it, I was immediately and completely in love.

It took methodical and persistent pestering, but I knew, inevitably, I would get on a plane by myself. And indeed I did. My parents got me a round-trip ticket from San Diego to Long Beach. It was only a seventeen-minute flight, but at age eleven it would serve its purpose. Relatives would pick me up in Long Beach and I would stay with them for a few days before returning home. I looked forward to seeing them, especially because they had a pool. For that reason they were always high on my list of people I liked to visit.

For the flight itself my parents also arranged, unbeknownst to me, for the stewardess—they were still called that in those days—to watch over me. Had I known of this, I would have been furious. I was a world traveler! I didn't need anyone hovering over me like I was a child. Later, my mother would say, "That's exactly why we didn't tell you about it."

So, wearing a pretty dress for the occasion, and carrying a little suitcase, I set off on my journey. Dad had instructed me on the best place to sit for the best view and most stable ride: right side in front of the wing. My face glued to the window, I sat transfixed by the blurring runway as we neared takeoff, and then suddenly my whole body was being pulled into the chair, the vibration under my feet disappeared, and we were airborne!

It was like the Peter Pan ride at Disneyland, the one where you're supposed to be flying at night above a town that's miniaturized by the alleged height, all twinkling lights thousands of feet below—except this was real and it was daytime.

Dad was right. Sitting in front of the wing my view was not obstructed. And since I could also look back to see the wing, I

knew I was not just on some sort of highly technical magic car-
pet, but was instead in the most remarkable machine I'd ever
experienced. It was mind-bogglingly wonderful, simply and
utterly glorious. There were landmarks I recognized, and sites
that would soon become landmarks, such as the construction for
Sea World. Everything spread out below us, but things were
going by too fast to take them all in.

And then the worst thing happened: not more than two minutes into the flight I got airsick. I'd never experienced that feeling before, the lightheadedness and my stomach doing back
flips all over my insides. I slumped down in my seat, craning
my neck to look outside beneath heavy eyelids. Everything
inside me screamed to throw up, but I refused. There was no
way this trip was going to be ruined by handing a used barf bag
to the nice stewardess.

She must have seen me turn green, because the next thing I
noticed was a cup of ginger ale attached to a finely manicured
hand. I looked over at her gratefully, and she smiled, full of pity
for my condition. "I'm fine," I croaked, taking the cup from her.

The nausea continued unabated until we began our descent
into Long Beach. There was nothing I wanted more intensely
than to be on that plane, but there I was, sick for almost the
entire trip. I was despondent. What cruel joke would make me
want so badly to fly, but then make me ill? There was a direct
relationship between the sheer thrill of flying and the sheer
awfulness of how I felt, and that relationship only increased in
intensity when I got on board the next plane to go home after a
nice week with my relatives—with whom I'd spent the first
twenty-four hours swigging Pepto Bismol, and then recovered
enough to spend countless hours in their pool.

There was no doubt in my mind, as I looked forward to the
ride home, that I would be flying again. My desire far outweighed

my nausea, though the latter had a good go as we took off from Long Beach.

Back in San Diego, I tottered off the plane and into my mother's arms, moaning, "I gotta go again."

"Oh, Meryl," she squeezed me impossibly tightly, "we missed you!"

"I wasn't gone for that long." I struggled to regain my breath.

"So," Dad said, giving me a little hug, "how was it? Got yourself a little airsick?"

How in the world could he tell? Would this mean I'd never be allowed to fly again? Impossible! "It was terrific!" I decided to be extra bright so he wouldn't remember later on. "I feel great. When can I go again?"

For weeks afterward I begged my father to take me on business trips with him. He often flew to Washington D.C. and other U.S. cities, and I could think of nothing better than tagging along with him. Of course I had to stay home and go to school, but Dad would always bring something back from his trips for us kids.

As soon as I returned from the Long Beach trip I immediately began plotting and planning a way to take another trip on my own. The wait nearly killed me. I knew this time it had to be to Europe; the Long Beach trip had just been for practice.

But my burning ambition to travel overseas—all on my own—was not to be realized for almost five years, until the very day I turned sixteen. By then I had it all worked out.

# CHAPTER 2

## Mr. Leon

Although my first flying experience had made me miserably ill, the flying bug had bitten me, and bitten hard. There was no amount of airsickness that would keep my feet on the ground for too long. Five years later I would find myself in the air once again.

By the time I was in junior high I was even more determined to fly again. This determination found new fuel when a school friend and her family took a trip to Switzerland. I plotted ways that I could trade places and go in her stead, justifying my deviousness with the fact that she, unbelievably, wasn't excited about going. In my book anyone who wasn't over the moon about traveling didn't deserve to go anywhere.

Needless to say, I didn't trade places with my girlfriend and was devastated at being left behind while she unenthusiastically traipsed off to Switzerland for the summer. For months after she got back I pumped her for information. What airline did they fly? How long was the flight? What cities did they stop in? Did they ride on trains much? Was it as beautiful as the pictures? What language was predominant? What time zone were they in? Was the food good? Did she visit a Swiss chocolate factory? And so on, *ad nauseum*.

I began to focus my feelings into action, manipulating my love of language to satisfy my craving for travel. For years I'd been interested in becoming fluent in German. So, with travel on my brain, I committed myself to further study. By the time I was a sophomore in high school, I decided it was time to get serious and go to Germany. After all, what better way to immerse oneself in the culture and truly learn the meaning and sense of the language beyond the textbooks?

It made perfect and complete sense to me, despite the fact that I had heated arguments with my ninth-grade German teacher, Mrs. Dalton, who opposed my studying abroad. I thought she had no sense of adventure at all. She insisted I was too young, and if I went at all it should be with a group. No way. I wanted total immersion and to travel alone, having to depend upon my own wits to fend for myself. I didn't want, need, or have the tolerance for a chaperone.

The next year I was in the tenth grade and attending Point Loma High School for the first time. There I had the good fortune to meet Mr. Ed Leon (pronounced Lay-*own*) for the very first time. I had a terrible crush on him and I wasn't alone. The girls loved him, the guys admired him and he was everyone's idol. Some people have a certain charisma or chemistry. Whatever you want to call it, he had it.

We students competed to get hired as his babysitter. He had five young children and a beautiful German wife named Marianne, whom we also came to know and admire. Mr. Leon wasn't just a friend and he wasn't just a teacher; he became my mentor and the most influential person in my life outside of my own parents.

One day early in the year I went to him and told him that, by the end of the academic year I planned to have rudimentary German behind me. That summer I would immerse myself completely in the language by going to Germany alone for the entire summer, and come back fluent. I was shocked when he agreed with me. Together with his support, my mom acknowledged the validity of the theory. There was only my dad left to conquer.

"No," my father said. He was sitting in the living room, just as he had during our last travel tussle, reading the paper.

"I've found the school."

"No."

"It's in Austria, actually—"

"No."

"— a language school, especially for learning German."

"No."

"Mr. Leon, my German teacher says it's a good school. He helped me research it."

"No."

"I've already got all the information," I thrust my hands out to him, pamphlets and paperwork slipping to the floor, "and I can stay with an Austrian family right by the school."

"No."

He would give in eventually. He had to. Mom had already agreed it was a good idea, despite the fact that neither one of them wanted their almost sixteen-year-old daughter traveling alone to Europe.

I spent the next several weeks arranging everything. I exhaustively researched flights and finally got a great deal with Atlantis Airlines, a West German charter airline flying out of San Diego to Frankfurt. It was Mr. Leon who found the school I would attend in Austria and who introduced me to the German-American Society of San Diego, which helped me find the terrific fare.   There was a family, the Jordans, who took in student boarders. They would be my host family, and because they didn't speak any English, I knew I would really be on my own. It was thrilling just thinking about it. From Frankfurt I would take a train to Innsbruck, Austria, where Herr Jordan was to meet me.

As much as I wanted to fly, I relished the idea of traveling the countryside by train, seeing it up close. Although I never dreamed of becoming a train engineer the way I would pursue becoming an airline pilot, I loved and was fascinated by trains, especially the idea of Old World travel through historic landscapes.

"No," my father said again as we drove to the airport the summer after my sophomore year of high school.

"No," continued as my parents walked me to the terminal.

"No," faded into my memory as I hugged them both and boarded the plane. My mother later told me that he continued to pound his fist into the palm of his hand with each emphatic "no" long after my plane receded into the distance.

I turned sixteen that day. I was ready to be thrust out into the world, completely on my own.

# CHAPTER 3

## Austria

The second flight of my life gave me no less airsickness than I'd experienced five years previously, but after a while I was able to overcome it. I learned later that it's not all that uncommon for some pilots to start out experiencing airsickness, but my case was far more intense than was the norm.

The flight itself was intoxicating and I began inflicting my German on the flight crew straightaway because they were all German. Well into the flight it suddenly occurred to me to ask about visiting the cockpit. The stewardess showed me in, where the captain welcomed my rapid-fire questions and clear awe of the plane's instruments. I couldn't believe how easy it was to gain admittance, and I felt immediately at home there, even though I understood virtually none of what I saw.

"How do you know what's for what?"

"This is what we train for." Then, turning to face me, he asked, "So, you like to fly?"

"No," I shook my head. "I *love* to fly. I could stay up here all the time."

"Well, maybe when you are done with school, you could become a stewardess."

"Mmm," I nodded, paying more attention to the vast expanse of sky and cloud out of the window. "How do you know how to navigate?"

The captain turned back to the instrument panel and pointed to a dial. "We navigate from fix to fix."

I had no idea what that meant, but I kept going. "And what about that?" I pointed to a small handle.

"That handle controls the wing flaps. They help us fly at slower airspeeds, like when we take off and land."

"Do you talk to the ground the whole time?"

"Pretty much. It varies depending on what airspace we are over."

"Where are we now?"

"We are just about to pass over Greenland." He pointed out his window. "You can see the coastline right there." It was night, but we were so far north it was not completely dark. Strangely, I hadn't felt sick at all in the cockpit.

I proceeded to ask about a hundred more questions before the stewardess came to get me. If she hadn't, I would have stayed up with the flight crew the whole trip.

I spent the rest of the night looking out the window for signs of water below, wondering how the pilot knew when to make the small turns I would feel once in a while. While everyone else slept, I was wide-awake, my face against the window. I wasn't going to miss a second of everything that was happening.

Dawn broke as we came in sight of the coast of Ireland. I was back in the cockpit and had a perfect view of my first experience of Europe. It was as enthralling as I'd expected, the coastline hazy in the morning sun.

We landed smoothly in Frankfurt and I found my way to the train station. It was amazing, with dozens and dozens of tracks with destinations all over Europe. I was enthralled just reading the names. Eventually, I found my train to Innsbruck. My first time on European soil!

As I settled into the rhythm of the train, I began to doze off.

I'd had no sleep on the airplane, anxious as I was not to miss anything, and now I was too exhausted to stay awake no matter how hard I tried. Every time I nodded off, a passing train would snap me awake, the explosive noise just a few feet away practically giving me a heart attack. The German gentleman sitting across from me in the compartment was sympathetic to my exhaustion but couldn't help laughing at the sight of my head sagging, then jerking upright with each passing train, then sagging again.

By the time my train reached Innsbruck that night the station was empty. I stood on the platform with my bag, wondering what to do next. The air, cool for June, perked me up, and I headed into the station lobby and sat down to wait. I thought I might call the Jordans to see if they were still coming to get me, but soon enough a man entered with a fatherly look of concern. I got up and introduced myself.

The Jordans' home in the foothills of the Alps was a narrow, three-story dwelling, typical of the Austrian Alps, with flower boxes at every window. Frau Jordan emerged from the kitchen. She was of medium build, like her husband, and she welcomed me warmly. Before leaving me to settle in, Frau Jordan told me that I could see the ski jump from the 1964 Winter Olympics across the valley clearly during the day from my bedroom window. I knew already I would love my time in Austria.

The next morning I decided to take a photograph of the Jordans' house and the mountains beyond it. The scenery was breathtaking. Backing up to fit everything into the frame, I stepped into some shrubbery. Not realizing it disguised the edge of a steep cliff, I tried to fit in one more step back.

Just then, the gravel and loose dirt gave way, and I began to fall, stopping an otherwise fatal drop off the side of the hill by grabbing onto a rose bush. Instantly, dozens of thorns drove deep into my hand. In my other hand I clutched my camera. I looked down and was horrified to see a sheer drop of around one hundred and fifty feet to a yard below. Slowly, painfully, I was able to kick a foothold into the side of the hill and make my way back onto firm ground.

Frau Jordan met me at the door as I stumbled in, covered in dirt and weeds. Thorns were embedded in my hand and my legs. Only my camera came away unscathed. Frau Jordan, who, it turned out, was once a nurse, looked at the blood gushing from my leg and beckoned me to the bathroom. For three hours she cleaned up my wounds, carefully pulling out each and every thorn with tweezers. It was excruciating, but at least it kept my mind off the blood still gushing from the deep chunk missing from my shin. Eventually, she stopped the bleeding. When she was finished, she simply smiled and patted me on my arm. I'm not sure why she didn't ask me what happened, but I was glad she hadn't; I was horribly embarrassed and extremely grateful to her for patching me up. At least I got my picture.

The city of Innsbruck was absolutely gorgeous, the name meaning "Bridge over the Inn," "Inn" being the name of the river and "bruck" meaning "bridge." The river was fast and full from the snow melting off the Alps, the water a most beautiful and opaque turquoise.

The school was a modern building among the otherwise ancient architecture. All the students were foreigners from a variety of countries, and we weren't allowed to speak unless it was in German. For three months I was completely immersed in another language and another culture. When I wasn't in school or hanging out with my new Austrian friends, I was hiking the incredibly beautiful Alps, spending time with my lovely host family, or exploring the many churches with their beautiful pipe organs, many times catching a concert or practice session.

The opportunity to meet new people from different countries was terribly exciting and I used the opportunity to try picking up phrases here and there in different languages. There were a couple of girls from Sweden, sisters named Kerstin and Eva, who taught me quite a bit of Swedish. I wrote home, "I know the months, the days, the numbers from one to one hundred, and quite a few useful phrases. I also know three *very* helpful words: one means 'damn,' another 'hell' and still another one that fortunately has no translation. Kerstin taught me all three words today when she caught her high-heel between two cobblestones." As I'd suspected, there was no substitute for hands-on learning.

On weekends the school arranged a wonderful variety of field trips. We drove through the Italian Alps to Venice, also a stunning visual experience. Venice itself was beautiful, but very, very hot. The water was of course undrinkable, Coke was a couple of bucks for just a few ounces, and the only thing we students could afford to drink was beer and wine, which was plentiful and cheap. I didn't even like it, but there was nothing else readily available. I tried not to think what my parents would say if they saw what I was swigging over there, but it couldn't be helped and I knew they would understand. Above all else, the respect of my parents was of paramount importance to me.

Another weekend we went to Switzerland. In a letter to my family I wrote, "Switzerland was lovely. It was sunny but cool and the country is really beautiful. Mom, Switzerland has the *sweetest* little cows. They were grazing by the side of the road and they all smiled and rang their cowbells as we went past. On the way back they were all walking along the road to their house, and we drove right through the middle of the herd. I saw a darling little mountain goat on the way back, too." Not exactly Hemingway, but I wrote home extensively and wanted to convey the beauty and delight I felt as much as possible.

My mother had urged me to keep a journal. I tried, but was not faithful about it. Much later she presented me with a packet of every letter I wrote home from all of my travels, saying knowingly, "For when you write your book." Mothers are exceedingly smart—especially mine.

During another field trip I discovered that the Danube River has a number of locks that allowed our boat to cruise from Linz to Vienna, where I was thrilled to recognize the scenery from one of my favorite films, *Almost Angels*, about the Vienna Boys Choir. (During the writing of this book, I was enchanted to speak with several current members of the choir when we crossed paths at Dulles Airport.) On a trip to Salzburg I got to see Mozart's house, and landmarks from *The Sound of Music*, another favorite of mine.

Music continued to be an important and prevalent ingredient in my life that summer. To my delight, I learned that Herr Jordan played the zither, a flat, stringed instrument. Although I played the guitar a little, I found the zither infinitely more difficult. Herr Jordan often invited me to play music with him, and sometimes friends would come over and accompany him on the guitar and mandolin. I would join in, and Herr Jordan was pleased that I already knew quite a few traditional German songs. He even taught me a few more. I was in heaven.

One song in particular enchanted me and I spent all summer practicing on Herr Jordan's zither, vowing to learn to play it. My rendition of it was nothing like Herr Jordan's, but I did learn the piece, practicing so long and so hard I got painful cramps in my wrists, which before then I hadn't known was possible.

At the end of my stay with the Jordan family, Herr Jordan insisted on giving me his zither, made of lovely deep-colored rosewood—a family heirloom. "It comes long way in my family," he smiled at me warmly, trying English for the first and only time of my visit.

"I can't take this," I clutched my heart. "It's been in your family—"

"—I want you to have it," he said, nodding for emphasis as he placed it in my hands. I still have the beautiful piece today, and cherish the Jordan family heirloom that has been entrusted to me.

In German-language school, I made new and lasting friends from a number of different countries. In fact, because the students were from all over the world, I was able to learn a bit about a number of other cultures.

I was surprised and pleased when my Dad showed up for a visit. He had written he'd be on a business trip to Zurich and would arrive by train. This was mid-summer, and by then I'd "gone native." I was dressed to the hilt looking as Austrian as possible in a dirndl I'd bought my very first day there. It had a red vest, blue skirt and flowered apron and I still have it. Many of the local women, including Frau Jordan, chose to wear this traditional dress for their everyday clothes and I often wore mine around town and when I went walking through the Alpine meadows just above the Jordans' house.

My Dad and I had dinner that night with Frau and Herr Jordan in the old part of Innsbruck at a wonderful restaurant overlooking the fast-flowing Inn River, and afterwards went to a floor show of traditional folk-dancing, the male dancers impossibly fast as they slapped their shoes and hands during the "schuhplattler." For some reason the Master of Ceremonies came to our table and asked who we were, and then introduced my Dad and me to the audience as a "famous scientist and his daughter from America." It was a little embarrassing, but at the time there simply weren't many Americans around and we were a novelty. I made an effort to look as intellectual as possible until the spotlight was off us and back on the dancers again.

The next evening my Dad, along with his friend and business associate who had come to pick him up for the drive back to Zurich, was treated to some of Frau Jordan's famous cooking along with her homemade dandelion wine. I had arranged an entourage of several cars for my Dad and his friend as they left town after dinner to make sure they got headed in the right direction; it was somewhat confusing entering and leaving Innsbruck by car. When we finally saw them off, there was a great honking of horns from the little parade which escorted them to the outskirts of town.

My Dad, who had been so worried about his "little girl" going to Europe alone, felt better, I'm quite sure, after meeting my wonderful host family and some of my friends from school. I was proud to be able to show off at least one of my parents to my host family and friends. With his warm manner and efforts to speak German as much as possible, he was a huge hit with everyone. As much as I was enjoying my independence, I was sad to see him go.

There was a girl from Paris, Anne-Marie Frappin, who also stayed at the Jordans' house that summer, and we became great friends. "When you go home," Anne-Marie advised me, "you should study French. Then next year you can come to visit me in Paris."

"Yes, yes," I agreed enthusiastically, "and you should come to America." A few years later, she did just that, staying with me and my family in San Diego.

"Since we're already on this continent, maybe you should come with me to Paris once first. You know," she laughed, "for practice." And so we did.

Anne-Marie had a car and one weekend we just took off. Once in Paris, I was hooked. At the time I didn't know anything about the French language other than a few key phrases my friends had taught me. Whereas German had always sounded familiar to me, French sounded completely incomprehensible. Nevertheless, I decided I must become fluent in French as quickly as possible. I hadn't even returned home yet, but already knew it was time to get to work on my next trip—I was going to come back just as quickly as I could manage. But first there was going to be a little side trip.

## CHAPTER 4

# Israel

That fall, back at Point Loma High School in San Diego, I entered the eleventh grade and enrolled in First Year French. After fearing I'd never grasp it, I was thrilled when I discovered how naturally it came to me. My teacher was an absolutely wonderful lady—a French Canadian named Mademoiselle Marie Lambert—and under her guidance I was able to start speaking French around the house the very first day.

Although I'd learned only a couple of key phrases from my French friends in Austria, they had insisted I get the pronunciation of the difficult French "r" correct. Those few phrases I learned were an important foundation to me, and later I won a small award in a citywide competition for the best French language pronunciation.

As certainly as I knew I would return to Europe the next summer—specifically France—I also knew I simply couldn't wait until then. I signed on through my Sunday school for a two-week trip to Israel during the winter break. I'd made a habit of taking on odd jobs to at least help pay for trips I knew I'd have to take, and doubled my efforts once the decision was made to go to Israel. I acted as responsibly as I could in all matters, always got the best deals on fares, never ever spent any allowance money other than on these trips, and earned extra money tutoring other students in German or doing housework, or whatever else I could find to earn some extra cash.

Although tensions were especially high in Israel and the Middle East in general during 1969-1970 and my father was once again forbidding me to go—a directive he knew would not be heeded—my grandmother thought it was right for me to visit my ancestral homeland. I, however, was far more excited about the prospect of traveling to a new and exciting destination, regardless of my familial connection to it.

About eight of us, including our Sunday school teacher, headed off to Israel in mid-December. On Christmas Eve, I rode a camel to Bethlehem, and later swam in the Red Sea near Eilat, a little settlement along the shore marking the border between Israel and Jordan. The water was an intensely dark blue and breathtakingly beautiful.

There was a sign on the beach with a skull and crossbones warning swimmers in seven languages not to drift into Jordan. I could read three. After swimming we took a glass-bottom boat on a tour in much deeper water and I was horrified to realize that I had shared the water with quite a few poisonous sea creatures.

We visited some Bedouin settlements and I was astonished to see that, in the middle of the desert, they kept ducks—mallards, to be exact. The Bedouins lived in tents and of course were accustomed to their own way of life, but ducks need water and I couldn't believe they could even survive with nowhere to swim.

At home in San Diego I had an adorable pet mallard named Meredith. She had been small enough to fit in the palm of my hand when my mother gave her to me one Easter. We kept a child's wading pool for her at the house, but she and I swam in every conceivable body of water in the San Diego area. She would body-surf in the waves right next to me down at Ocean Beach, come swimming with me in Mission Bay and the beach areas on Shelter Island—all over the place. She would have been one unhappy duck without plenty of opportunities to swim.

After visiting the Bedouins, we went on to the Dead Sea and the Sea of Galilee before heading home—it was like a Tour of the Seas, though as an avid swimmer and water lover, I didn't mind. I not only didn't mind, I was ecstatic; this was one of the best parts of the trip.

I didn't experience a particular religious awakening, but was awed nevertheless by the tradition and history everywhere around me. I was also mindful of the continuing crisis the people of that region face. In Jerusalem, the windows in our hotel had been blown out, leaving our rooms freezing cold in the December air, and we heard gunshots in the streets every night. In Tel Aviv a bomb went off next door.

I decided I didn't need to mention the bombings and shootings to my parents when I got home. They were already stressed enough. Honestly, I don't know to this day how I got away with so much travel so early on, especially to a place such as Israel, always inherently vulnerable to violence. The only saving grace was that this particular time—and only this time—I wasn't traveling alone. They had objected strenuously, of course, but I was younger and had more stamina than they did.

On the New Year's Eve return flight from Tel Aviv to New York, with a stop in Paris, I felt no airsickness. The night sky was gloriously clear, and all the passengers were in a celebratory mood. Everyone stayed awake and the champagne flowed each time the captain announced New Year's as we passed through the different time zones. Although I didn't feel the nausea of airsickness, I didn't manage a healthy flight. Instead, I began coming down with a bad cold, and midway over the Atlantic, I developed a full-blown fever.

At JFK Airport in New York we left El Al Airlines and went through customs. I tried to look as healthy as possible for the Health and Immigration folks. Before boarding the United Airlines DC-8 to Los Angeles, I went outside and knelt in the snow to help curb my nausea and cool off from the intense fever I was running.

The New Year's Day flight was sparsely populated and the stewardesses moved me up to First Class, where they made me as comfortable as possible. Wrapped in airline blankets, I shivered back to the west coast. The best part of it all, though, was the United captain who came back especially to see me and ask how I was feeling. At that moment, I was on top of the world, fever, nausea and all. I was flattered and moved almost to tears at the captain's fatherly concern at my illness as he tucked me in with a blanket. Later on, the memory of this flight and this particular pilot would influence my decision to make United my first choice of airlines, both as a passenger and as a pilot.

# CHAPTER 5

## France

As it happened, the same people who ran the school in Austria also ran one in Montpellier, in the south France on the Mediterranean Sea, west of the Riviera. I made arrangements to stay in Paris at the flat of my friend Anne-Marie—whom I'd met in Austria on my first European trip—for a couple of weeks before heading to school.

The spring semester of my junior year did not go by fast enough, but finally I was headed to Paris. Anne-Marie made plans to stay with a friend in order to give me full use of her ninth-floor walk-up at 5 Place d'Italie. The flat was tiny, what I thought of as an "artist's garret." There was a bed under a slanted window-roof and just a cold-water sink for bathing and cooking, which was done on a hotplate. The toilet was a hole in the floor in a room down the hall. I couldn't have been more delighted; I wasn't looking for a five-star hotel, I was looking for independence and adventure, and I got it!

The moment I walked in the door I felt at home. For the first few days in Paris I barely slept. How could I? There was too much to see, too much to do and, unfortunately, way too much to eat. Every morning I set off in a different direction: to the Louvre, the Eiffel Tower, Notre Dame. I walked everywhere initially, then later on became an expert at riding the

Metro—my first subway experience. I was horrified at the manner in which the French simply threw their ticket stubs on the ground after they were used. I hated litter, but Anne-Marie just laughed when I expressed dismay.

Generally, though, I loved the French and was unabashed about faking my way in the language as much as possible with my first year of academic French now behind me. They appreciated it and went out of their way to be helpful to me. With Anne-Marie's guidance I saw many local haunts. We hung out in cafés like Left Bank intellectuals and browsed the art stalls that lined smaller streets.

One day, as we admired a painter's work, he asked me if he could paint me. I was utterly taken aback. But then I looked at the lovely paintings—and to Anne-Marie for approval—and we headed back to Henri's studio.

Once there, however, I got cold feet. "I don't know about this, Anne-Marie," I whispered as Henri set up his materials. "I've never posed for a painting before. I don't know this guy."

"De rien," she dismissed my concern. "It is nothing. Henri will tell you what he wants. Right, Henri?"

"Bien sûr!" he agreed jovially.

Then she began parading about the flat, striking exaggerated poses and sucking in her cheeks to create ridiculous faces. By the time Henri was ready to paint, I was exhausted from laughing so hard, feeling far too giddy to worry over posing for a painting. Henri created a number of portraits in that one sitting.

And so I added modeling for a French painter to my growing list of adventures. A few days later, as I prepared to leave for Montpellier, I saw my paintings in some of the merchants' stalls along the Seine.

From Paris I boarded a train and was met in Montpellier by my host family, also non-English speaking. As with the school in Austria, this one arranged wonderful excursions on weekends—to the beaches of the Riviera, to the famous Pont du Gard, the famous three-tiered aqueduct over the Rhône River, where we swam underneath in the crystal clear water, to the home of Picasso, to vineyards and all over the French countryside. Many weekends I spent at the nearby beaches swimming in the beautiful, warm, clear waters of the Mediterranean Sea.

I'm afraid I did not behave myself at all and gained about twenty pounds that summer. Upon my return home I went on a diet immediately. I was horrified at the weight gain, but it certainly was fun eating my way around France—all the way until I had to face the reality of the scale.

The headmaster of the school offered an extra course—an introduction to Russian. Previously, Mr. Leon had undertaken teaching me some Russian after school, and, like German and French, I loved it. With its different alphabet, certainly it was the most challenging of the three languages, but I didn't find it all that difficult and was immensely intrigued by it. At my French school, I was one of the few takers for the Russian course, and was able to get to a point of basic conversational Russian. That of course got me to thinking: where would my travels take me next?

## CHAPTER 6

## Russia!

Before I'd returned from France the summer prior to my senior year in high school, I'd already decided a trip to the Soviet Union would be my high school graduation present to myself. Although correctly referred to as the Soviet Union, it was generally referred to as just "Russia." I did manage to stay in San Diego my entire senior year in high school—no easy feat for me. But I was so entranced by all the doors that had been opened to me merely by learning other languages, that I decided more must be better. I proceeded to sign up for adult night school every night that language classes were offered: Monday through Thursday.

I was now taking advanced German and French in high school during the day, having pretty much skipped right out of the basic language programs, while at night I was taking Italian, Japanese, Russian and Spanish. It was surprising to my peers that I wasn't more proficient in Spanish, the language considered easiest to learn by most Americans. But Spanish held no charm for me. It wasn't nearly exotic enough—not the language of a far away land. We were, of course, very near Tijuana, on the border of Mexico, so I thought of Mexico more in terms of being just another neighborhood rather than another country.

My parents, incidentally, had no problem with my taking so many language courses. My school counselor, though, did have a problem with it, unduly worried that I had no social life.

"Meryl, why are you doing this?" she asked, folding her hands on top of her desk. "Don't you ever have any fun?"

*Let's see now*, I thought. *I am a senior in high school and have already been overseas three times. Yes, I am having fun!* I had to temper my answer as I thought she was a complete imbecile for thinking what I was doing wasn't fun. What did she think I should be doing, attending more football games on Friday nights? "Are you kidding?" was all I could say to her at first. Then I gathered my composure and continued. "This *is* my idea of fun. The classes I want to take are not all classroom lessons. Look." I showed her the school catalogues. "See? They teach you songs and about the cultures and food and all sorts of interesting things."

"Don't you ever date?" she asked.

*What in the world has* that *got to do with anything?* I thought, annoyed. "Yes, once, for the junior prom and it was so horrible that I don't even want to go to my senior prom. I do stuff with the German Club and the French Club all the time, though. Does that help you out at all?" I tried not to sound too sarcastic.

"I can't let you do it," she said.

"But why?" I pleaded. "What's the actual reason? Because you think I should date more?"

"I just know the rest of your school load will suffer. That's six languages you'll be studying at the same time. You just can't do it. It's too much. Surely your parents can't approve of this."

"Listen," I said, leaning forward in my chair. "My parents absolutely do approve. I'm fluent in French and German now and it's just a fact that learning languages this easily is a gift. I want to exploit it as much as possible. Why don't we do this: I'll make an extra effort in all my other classes and if I get straight "A's" after the first semester, I get to continue. I reserve the right to not get an "A" in gym, however." Athletics never was my strong point.

She sighed, but finally said, "Get me a note from your parents. Put what you just said in writing, and you have my approval—with reservations."

I was ecstatic and went to my night classes. There were thirteen grades on my report card that semester—all A's, even in gym. Looking back, it amazes me how intent some adults were in stifling my almost insatiable urge to learn more. I didn't get it then and I don't get it now.

Naturally, with Russian as my new primary focus, my senior year included research on a trip to the Soviet Union. It was out of the question this time to find a school that would allow its foreign students to stay with host families; that was not permitted in the Soviet Union.

Once again it was Mr. Leon who found the school I would attend that summer, at a place called "Dyuny" (rhymes with "puny"), which means "dunes." Situated north of Leningrad on the Gulf of Finland—right on the beach—where there were, indeed, sand dunes, Dyuny would prove to be beautiful.

I would fly to Frankfurt once again, this time staying overnight with a young, non-English speaking German woman named Ingrid in her flat at 84 Darmstädter Landstrasse. A mutual friend had put me in touch with her and Ingrid had subsequently invited me to stay with her in Frankfurt whenever I was passing through. In fact, I was to stay with her on numerous occasions during my travels in the coming years.

Once again, I found myself standing before my father as he sat in his chair with the requisite paper, my hands folded neatly in front of me. I cleared my throat. Then I cleared it again.

He put the paper down and looked at me. "I know what those hands mean," he said evenly, "and the answer is no."

Smiling sweetly, I began the slow, inexorable wearing away that would result in his acquiescence—or at least his not standing in my way. "I was talking to Mom and Mr. Leon—"

"—this is not a majority-rule decision."

"But you have no idea what I'm going to ask."

"Language school in Russia."

I was impressed, but taken off-guard. This one was already not going quite as I'd expected. Though I knew I'd hear the requisite "no," I hadn't planned on him knowing what I was going to do.

"I'm not obtuse, Meryl." I opened my mouth to speak, but he cut me off before I could get started. "Israel was bad enough. Do you have *any* idea what you're talking about? This is the *Soviet Union. You* are an *American.* Do you see the difficulty?"

"Oh, well," I waved my hand, "Mr. Leon has that all worked out."

He was unimpressed. "Really."

I nodded enthusiastically.

"No."

"Dad, come on!"

"No."

"Honestly! Mom said—"

"No."

"No, Mom didn't say no, actually, she—"

"You've heard of Stalin, right? I mean, you're not entirely unaware of what you're trying to do."

"Oh Dad, Stalin's not worried about little old me. Besides, isn't he dead?"

"You're not going."

I sighed.

"No."

"But I didn't even *say* anything!"

He arched an eyebrow. "You don't have to."

At least I'd started early. I had a few good months left to wear him out. Among the many wonderful attributes of my father are his belief that I am capable of anything, and his insistence on trying to keep me safe. The former instilled in me the courage to try everything I've ever dreamed of doing, while the latter gave me the opportunity to practice overcoming "no." If I hadn't had so much practice, I might not have learned to be an expert at finding the back or side door to every front door that was locked.

At the airport gate on the night I left for Frankfurt, my mom hugged me and reminded me to keep my traveler's checks in separate safety areas. She wagged a finger at me. "You never know."

"Don't worry, Mom," I said, giving her one last squeeze. Then I turned to my father. "I promise to call the moment I land. Promise."

He shook his head in defeat, murmuring, "No."

A quick peck on his cheek and I disappeared onto the plane. Settled in my seat, picked for perfect night viewing, I gazed out the window as the plane taxied away.

Take-off was always so exciting. The remarkable speed and lift required to hoist that much weight off the ground was astonishing to me. With the interior lights dimmed, the glow from San Diego precisely marked the line where land ended and the vast Pacific began. Once out over the ocean we circled back toward the city and headed east. I was on my way!

I stayed awake for most of the flight to Frankfurt. I also found my way, once again, into the cockpit, where the illumination was, for me, the equivalent of Christmas lights. It was, and still is, utterly magical to be up front in an airplane—day or night.

One thing I'd never done was taken an overnight train ride. I just had to experience this. So, upon arrival, I caught a train to Cologne, Germany, where I would switch to a train routed all the way to Moscow, through Poland—a three-day trip. I had a sleeper car, of course, which I shared with other passengers as they got on and off along the way. It wasn't a first class car with any privacy, just beds that folded up against the wall during the day. But bedding was handed out each night and I was torn between letting the cradling of the train's motion lull me to sleep in my bed or hanging out by the window all night. Sleep always won, eventually.

I was excited to be going through the Iron Curtain and through Poland, which had held a particular fascination for me ever since that fateful day when my mother introduced me to Polish folk music and the Polish State Folk Ballet.

I was taken aback, however, when Polish Border Guards boarded the train as we entered Poland, demanding our visas. I had my Russian visa, but hadn't known about needing a Polish one.

"Not worry," they laughed in thickly accented English. "Transit Visa only. You give us money, we give you visa."

What a relief. I'd thought for one scary moment I was going to get kicked off the train behind the Iron Curtain. That was in fact going to happen, but not this trip.

Stopping in Warsaw at sunset I saw the most incredible sight: the entire city somehow appeared as one big hill made of odd-sized houses and other buildings. I don't know how to describe it any differently. The whole scene had an unearthly glow about it.

My train crossed into the Soviet Union at the border town of Brest. Included in my preparations for my trip to Russia was stocking up on Levis jeans. I'd heard I could sell them in Russia on the Black Market for a tidy profit, which I could parlay into another trip. If nothing else, I have always been enterprising—so enterprising, in this case, that I knew enough to pack my suitcase when the time came with a cassette player placed indiscreetly at the top of my suitcase, on top of a heap of clothes. It was a decoy to throw the Russian customs guys off my jeans trail.

I'd learned from other people who'd traveled to Russia before me that American Levis were very hot property, but if you distracted the Soviet customs officers with a cassette or other recording device, you could slip them into the country undetected. After having so much travel experience behind me already, I felt emboldened to try my hand at it. I felt I was a regular James Bond with my decoy plan.

I was told that my cassette player would be catalogued and stored in a warehouse, and that I could retrieve it upon my return. All passengers who had illegal possessions confiscated were shown into a huge warehouse where there were thousands of items stocked on shelves all the way up to the ceiling. They even showed us the individual shelf on which our items were placed. Then they gave us claim tickets, as if they were checking our coats, and sent us back to the train.

As the train moved off toward Moscow, I smiled to myself, pleased with my ruse. There was no way I believed I'd ever see that cassette player again, but that was okay. I had three more just like it under the jeans. I understood cassette players also sold well.

It was still a very long way to Moscow, but I enjoyed my Russian train ride immensely. I had been warned in advance that passports would be collected at the border, which they were, and returned upon arrival in Moscow, which they were. It was still a little unsettling, though, to be inside the Soviet Union and not in possession of my passport. Along the way I learned to love Russian tea, made with water heated in the silver *samovar* in the corridor of each train car.

When my train finally arrived in Moscow, people in and around the station were openly distressed, and some were crying. After some inquiry I learned that three Russian cosmonauts were found dead in their seats after having landed from twenty-four days in space. Later I found out that the landing capsule had suffered a breach upon reentry, allowing air to escape and depressurize the cabin. Many of the people I'd seen during my brief experience with them looked hard or indifferent, but not that day. The grief in the air was overwhelming, with little wonder.

Most Soviets I met were not Communists. They distinguished sharply between themselves, as Russians, and the government, which was Communist. But the oppression of that ideology had seeped into even the most mundane of daily activities. I remember a vending machine that dispensed water into a cup. You'd drink out of it, return the cup, and then the machine would spray the cup with water to clean it until the next person happened by. I found that repugnant. Even if the cleaning water had been scalding hot—and there was no indication that it was—I couldn't believe people had to share cups for a simple glass of water.

Just when I thought I'd recovered from the water situation, something else happened that was just astonishing to me. I'd heard Russian ice cream was exceptionally good and couldn't wait to try it. I was shocked when a scoop of ice cream was placed directly into my outstretched hand along with a coarse sheet of paper meant to pass for a napkin. *Haven't these people ever heard of ice cream cones?* I thought. Apparently not. The ice cream was good, but after that I stuck to buying *Batons*, an ice cream treat somewhat like our Eskimo Pies, shaped like a small baton and wrapped in paper.

I also discovered the joys of chocolate butter, which sounded and looked simply disgusting but was actually quite good, and *kefir*, which I had for breakfast pretty much every day. It tasted quite a bit like buttermilk and was delicious with sugar. You can find flavored kefir in our stores here now, but at the time I didn't know what it was. Later during my trip I even had Chicken Kiev in Kiev! (I called my mom right afterwards to inform her that her Chicken Kiev was better, which was true.)

Another piece of culture shock was to be found deep below the streets in both Moscow and Leningrad, where each subway station looked like a palace. There were even shopping centers down there in some locations.

Transportation was amazingly cheap—three Kopeks (pretty much the same as three cents) for a bus, four for a streetcar and five for the subway.

Everything in Moscow felt big. The buildings, the doors, all of it heavy and large. Immovable, just like I imagined the people to be. Nobody was in a hurry to move because there was nothing to hurry to. The weight of the architecture just seemed to me to drive that point home. Nevertheless, the remnants of the old architectural designs were extraordinary. In the face of an otherwise dreary environment, the spirals and swirling church towers were practically whimsical.

I'd always wanted to see St. Basil's Cathedral in Red Square, commissioned in 1552 by Czar Ivan IV, otherwise known as Ivan the Terrible. It was just as impressive in real life as I'd imagined it would be from the pictures. I'd never realized that it was actually eight churches clustered around one central belfry.

For all the dourness of life in Moscow, I found people very excited to meet an American—and to purchase American jeans. I became very popular very quickly, and sold out of my Levis and cassette players before I'd even made it to school.

After a couple of days in Moscow seeing the sights, I took an Aeroflot plane to Leningrad (now St. Petersburg) known as the "Venice of the North" because of the numerous canals.

One night when I couldn't sleep, I went out walking very late and crossed the Neva River. What I didn't know was that the bridges, which were all drawbridges, came up and stayed up all night after about 11:00 PM.

When I decided it was time to return to my hotel, I discovered the bridges were up for the rest of the night and I was stuck on the wrong side of the river. Leningrad is far enough north that it wasn't completely dark, but it was still a little intimidating to know I had nowhere to go for the rest of the night.

I didn't know what to do, and so I approached a Russian policeman in a park. He laughed when I told him I was stranded, and told me I wasn't the first, and wouldn't be the last. He kindly took me back to his station, where I spent the night in an unused cell. They gave me a cot and a blanket and seemed quite amused at my predicament. But they were nice enough and in the morning they gave me tea and some pastry and I went on my way, no worse for having spent the night in a Russian jail.

From Leningrad I caught a bus up to Dyuny and school. It was right on the beach as I'd hoped, and also on the edge of a beautiful birch forest with lakes, streams and ponds—an absolutely gorgeous setting in which to further study the Russian language. The University of Leningrad hosted the school; it was some of their faculty that taught there during the summer.

Our class took several field trips—to Kiev, to the Summer Palace near Leningrad, and to Tbilisi, the capital of the Republic of Georgia—during my stay. We took a plane from Leningrad to Tbilisi. I was nauseous the whole trip but still managed to be awed by the beautiful Caucasus Mountains. The plane was very old and had windows you could open from the ceiling by means of a crank. The noise was horrific.

Obviously, with the windows open the plane wasn't pressurized and we didn't attain much altitude, maybe ten or eleven thousand feet. At the time I wondered if that was due to the enormity of the stewardesses. They were easily three hundred pounds, very scary, and provided terrific self-evidence that stewardesses need not be slight, lovely, or delicate. These women could just as well have hoisted the plane over their heads and hurled it over the mountains to Tbilisi. Nevertheless, they were very nice to me and the other students, even giving me an extra lemon drop for my airsickness. Everyone else got only one.

When the summer was over and it was time to return home, I once again flew to Moscow and from there boarded the train that would take me all the way back through Poland and then to Cologne for the transfer to Frankfurt and the flight home.

We stopped in Brest again, of course, and I half expected to have the customs officials laugh when I presented my claim ticket, but unbelievably, the cassette was just where I'd left it!

## CHAPTER 7

# A Very Red Army

Industriousness and curiosity—euphemisms, my father would say, for bull-headedness and reckless abandon—have been abiding characteristics of my personality. Recently, I found a letter from my old friend and high-school German teacher, Mr. Leon, in which he wrote, "I am convinced that you are a genius, and as a result, you are very creative. You will get what you want almost always." It might take some time, and I might have to overcome life's various obstacles, but, like the inexorable movement of time, inevitably I would triumph.

Now, I'm pretty sure I am not a genius, but I am nothing if not tenacious, and I do think that tenacity is one of several parents of creativity. Another parent is Obstacle, whose close relatives are Negativity and Discrimination. I'd met them before, in the various characters I'd come across, but until I was accidentally introduced to my career, I'd not really experienced them as an entire family. To be charitable to the people whose attitudes set obstacles in my path, it is a certainty that I would not have had as much adventure had I been able to take the direct route to where I am now.

Whether it was because I hadn't put two-and-two together, or because people just hadn't done the calculations much before, it hadn't yet occurred to me to combine my love of flying and travel into a career as an airline pilot. A typical example of my era might also help to explain why I'd not thought of, nor been encouraged to, pursue flying as a career.

I think it was in the fifth grade that our teacher was asking all the students what they wanted to be when they grew up. Some boys said doctors or lawyers or cowboys or plumbers. My friend, Marilyn, said she wanted to be a doctor. "No," the teacher corrected her, "You mean a nurse." Marilyn responded, politely but firmly, "No, I mean a doctor." The teacher gave her a surprised look and moved on. That little exchange made a huge impression upon me and I've never forgotten the sound in Marilyn's voice. Dr. Marilyn Thoman, last time I heard, was a prestigious cancer research scientist at the Sidney Kimmel Cancer Center in San Diego.

When I was asked the same question, I answered that I wanted to be an astronaut and go to the moon. Wordlessly, our teacher moved on to the next student.

Interestingly enough, as many people in positions of power as there have been who denied me over the years, I do not count my father among them. Any "no" was wholly and exclusively a "no" of love and care. If one door was closed, I'd go around to the back, and as often as not, there was someone there to unlock the door and let me in. Of course, sometimes I just busted the door down and walked on in. One thing I never did, however, was make a request or demand that I wasn't prepared to back up with know-how and experience. That's not to say, however, that I didn't also learn at times on the fly.

Upon my return from the Soviet Union, in my first year of college and first year of formal Russian language, I went to the San Diego City Schools board and offered my services as a teacher's aide—for pay, of course—in Russian, at the very high school from which I graduated, Point Loma High.

"But," one board member argued, "How can you teach a language in which you're not completely fluent?"

"Surely you know that when you learn a language, you begin with very elementary words and phrases, right?"

"Yes," she responded.

"Let me give you an example so you can see how I teach." I began giving them a beginning lesson, and by the end of our meeting, I not only had the job, but also had the whole board saying elementary phrases in Russian.

Fortunately for me, I also had the support and mentoring of Mr. Leon, along with my San Diego State Russian professor, Dr. Renate Bialy, whom I adored. She wrote a letter for me saying she thought my teaching the course was absolutely viable, and that my pronunciation was nearly perfect—certainly good enough to teach a beginning class for gifted students.

So I began taking Russian courses in the morning at college, and teaching students at my former high school in the afternoon, always keeping a step ahead. I remember the look on the face of the clerk at the college bookstore as I bought about twenty Russian textbooks, enough for my whole high school class.

In addition to Russian, I was also taking several other language courses. My plan was to learn as many languages as possible, and travel, travel, travel—which really meant fly, fly, fly! The language part was going fine, but, as is typically the case, my college years were lean ones, so I wasn't expecting travel to be much in my picture.

Nevertheless, I did get in one trip to Russia that winter, and one more trip the summer after my freshman year: a camping trip with some fellow college students for which we rented a Volkswagen van and drove across northern Europe, into the Soviet Union, south through Romania and Bulgaria, then up through Yugoslavia, Hungary, Czechoslovakia and back where we'd started.

I left on the winter trip during the first winter break in college ostensibly to study more closely the language in its natural environment. I took the same route as I had the previous summer, starting in Frankfurt and taking the three-day train ride all the way to Moscow, wanting to experience everything I'd seen before, but in winter this time. I also brought more jeans, and, of course, the sacrificial cassette.

I was bundled up to the hilt, but even so, when I got to Moscow, it was so cold I understood at once what all the Russian resignation was about. With some of my jeans earnings I purchased two balalaikas, triangular guitar-like instruments, one for me and one for a friend of mine back home.

Somehow, when it was time to get back on the train for Frankfurt, I managed to board the wrong one. Okay, that's not entirely true—at least, it wasn't quite as vague as all that. Being a rather self-sufficient and experienced traveler by that point in my life, I can't simply say that I sort-of-kind-of-happened-to get on the wrong train. There was a young man.

While waiting for my Frankfurt train I met a very handsome young army officer. Red Army. Now, I didn't just follow him onto the wrong train like a puppy. We'd been chatting and flirting—he looked quite good in his uniform—when I asked which one was the train to Berlin. Forgetting for the moment to consider where I was, I assumed I'd be shown the train to *West* Berlin. My handsome Soviet officer, on the other hand, was naturally thinking *East* Berlin. And so he said, with a smile that anticipated further conversation with me during the ride, that I should follow him. So I did.

I found myself on a train full of Red Army officers, about thirty of them, headed to East Berlin. By the time I realized what I'd done, it was too late. The train was not only moving—we'd already been traveling for several hours. There was nothing to do about it by the time I realized my mistake, so I figured I could change trains somewhere along the way. I figured wrong, of course.

As the sun set, the Red Army officers began drinking vodka, which led to someone pulling out a balalaika, which in turn led to someone singing. Naturally, I had to join in with one of my own balalaikas. I was welcomed heartily and the men were delighted when they heard I could play traditional folk tunes and even knew words to some songs in Russian. As the night wore on the playing got more rambunctious and the singing got louder. Thinking back, I imagine looking through the windows as the train rolled by, seeing a load of drunken Red Army men and one slight American girl, all of whom are playing and singing with furious abandon.

One by one the boys dropped off until only a few of us were left to play quietly at the back of the car. The most amazing thing of all, though, was what they wore to sleep. For a moment I thought *I* was the one who'd been imbibing too much vodka, for I swear the Red Army officers wore red long johns! Everywhere I looked there was red underwear sprawled about the car. I took that—and fatigue—as my cue to find a different car for the rest of the ride.

When we arrived in East Berlin late at night, some of my new Red Army friends delivered me to the border, where I'd have to walk from East Berlin through the Berlin Wall to West Berlin. I had come through Checkpoint Charlie coming the other way, a stopping point established for Westerners so they knew that they were leaving the American Sector of Berlin and going behind the Iron Curtain.

This time it was just the East Germans and me. I explained to them that I'd gotten on the wrong train. I also had to explain

my balalaikas, which were "dressed" in several layers of shirts
I'd used to protect them from scratching and to make more
room in my suitcase. Balalaikas come in all different sizes;
some so large they have to be rested on the floor when played.
The balalaikas I'd bought were the size of mandolins—rounded
on the back and flat on the front, so they were most easily carried bundled face-to-face.

"Dead bodies," I laughed, gesturing at the clothed figures.
Apparently the East-German-Border-Boys were appointed
based upon their complete and utter lack of humor, and I was
the only one who laughed. I was told sternly to "undress" my
balalaikas for inspection, and then of course I was stuck dress-
ing them back up again. I sighed inwardly and did as I was told.

Because the Russian Red Army train did in fact terminate in
East Berlin, and it was the middle of the night, there was no
hope of catching another train any time soon. I had to walk to
West Berlin. How very spooky to walk right through the Berlin
Wall to freedom, knowing *I* could do it but those I rode the train
with could not—at least, not without being shot.

It wasn't very far, but it was after all winter and bitterly
cold. I hauled my suitcase and "dead bodies" and slinked across
the border in the dead of night, leaving the glare of the East
German border searchlights behind.

Once there, I made my way to the train station in West
Berlin but realized I had absolutely no idea what to do next.
Inside the station was a poster of one of the most famous casu-
alties of World War II, the burned out church in West Berlin—
the Kaiser Wilhelm-Gedächtnis-Kirche. I stood gazing at it,
wondering what to do for the next few hours until the train station woke up again.

A clean-cut station agent with a gentle countenance
approached me and asked in German what had happened that I

was in that deserted station in the middle of the night. When I explained, he offered me shelter for the next few hours of darkness in the basement of the train station. There was a "drunk tank" there, kind of like our Salvation Army, and I climbed into the upper bunk over a derelict sleeping off his booze and snoring loudly.

In the morning they fed me coffee and pastries, and from there I was able to catch a train the rest of the way to Frankfurt for the flight home. During the ride, it occurred to me to wonder whether other train stations had such facilities, but I am happy to report I never had occasion to find out. At least I had obtained useful information and now knew where to go were I ever to get seriously drunk in West Berlin.

# Chapter 8

## Learn to Fly!

By the time I was a junior in college, I was on my way to majoring in Linguistics with a minor in Music. One day during the winter quarter, as I was taking a seat in Hebrew class—my thirteenth foreign language —I noticed a poster. Typically I didn't pay attention to flyers, but this one was different; it had a picture of a prop-plane on it. "Private Pilot Ground School—Learn to Fly!" it commanded. But of course! Why hadn't I thought of that before? Of course I should learn to fly. It hit me, right then and there. I was going to be an airline pilot! Why, why, why had this never occurred to me before?

Until that day I'd never cut class. But this was different. I *had* to go, had to with the same urgency I'd felt years before when I had to fly and travel overseas. There was no denying this sudden and unexpected compulsion. "One Poster, One New Career," a newspaper headline about me would later read.

I frantically jotted down the information, gathered up my books and took off for the administration building to sign up. In some sense it was natural that I'd not thought before of becoming a pilot. Though I grew up with aviation in my blood, learning how to pilot planes just wasn't common knowledge. There were no flight schools to speak of in the way that there are law schools and medical schools, and I'd never actually met a pilot on a social basis whom I could talk to about flying.

There had previously been no courses at all related to aviation at San Diego State College (not yet San Diego State University), and there were to be just two aviation classes offered through their Extension Program—Airport Management and Private Pilot Ground School.

I certainly had no interest in managing an airport, but seeing that poster caused a major shift in my entire consciousness—if it had any relationship to aviation whatsoever, I was interested. So I signed up on the spot for both classes. I knew this was a major turning point for me. Languages, for the first time, were about to take a back seat.

Both extension classes were to be held in offices at Montgomery Field in San Diego. The first class was Airport Management. I don't remember much about that class other than the first night. I was sitting next to a guy who turned out to be a San Diego policeman *with his own plane!*

We were gathering up our stuff to leave when he introduced himself. "I'm Frank Knight." He held out his hand.

I took it. "Meryl Getline."

I was the only girl in the class as well as the youngest person, and most of the twenty or so guys there made it a point to introduce themselves. That was my first inkling that I was about to enter an almost exclusively male environment, which was fine with me. The difficulty of doing so, however, would become apparent soon enough.

"If you'd like to go up, I'll take you." He smiled.

"How? I mean, yes, I'd love to! But how?"

"I've got my own plane, a Cherokee, right here."

"That's fantastic, yes!" I had no idea what a Cherokee was, but it didn't matter. So long as it took me up in the air, I was happy. "Wait, when?"

"How about right now?"

"You're kidding! Really?"

"Sure."

"But it's almost nine o'clock. Don't you need to get going?"

"Doesn't matter. I don't mind staying up late if you don't."

"No! Of course I don't mind! Let's go!"

We drove over to where his plane was parked on the other side of the field. It was a beautiful, single-engine Piper Cherokee. He did the requisite walkaround, explaining what he was doing—checking tire pressures, oil level, general condition—things like that. We got in and I was amazed at what looked to me at that time like an impossibly vast array of instruments. I had no idea what anything was for, and I felt a sense of panic. How in the world did one learn all of this? Was I really capable of it?

Frank must have seen the look on my face. "It's really not hard once you get the hang of it," he offered.

"Sure, Frank, whatever you say."

"No, I'm serious. You'll get it."

"Okay, would you take just one instrument—an easy one—and tell me exactly what it does?"

Pilots, as it turns out, seem to be born instructors. When people express any interest whatsoever, they're usually happy to demonstrate their knowledge. My level of interest was intense, to say the least, and Frank carefully chose about five different items and explained them in depth.

I mentally breathed a sigh of relief. It didn't seem that hard once he explained everything. At least, it seemed do-able. There was just an enormous amount to learn and I was absolutely aching to get started. I wanted to know everything—right now!

We took off, my very first takeoff with a cockpit view, and I was enthralled. It was pitch-black that night and quite late by the time we got airborne, so traffic was minimal. There was some radio conversation and I strained to understand, but much of it was incomprehensible to me. *Like learning another language*, I thought. *Right up my alley.*

I will never, ever forget the magic of that first night-flight. I felt exhilarated beyond what I thought possible. This was it! This was my calling, and everything else I had ever done had led to this moment.

We even flew over to Lindbergh Field and shot some touch-and-goes, where you touch down, reconfigure your flaps, and take off again without slowing down all the way.

There was a Delta Airlines jet waiting for take-off as we came in. It hadn't occurred to me that a little airplane like Frank's was just as entitled to use a main airport like Lindbergh Field as the "big boys." But they are, and I got my first true taste of aviation that night.

I got home very late that night. I had called home to let my mother know I'd been invited up in an airplane, and she was in bed reading but awake and waiting for me. My father was out of town.

As I practically glided into their bedroom, she said, "Honey, if I didn't know better, I'd say you were high on drugs. Your feet aren't even touching the floor!"

I said, "Mom! Guess *what?* I'm going to be an airline pilot!"

And my sweet ever-lovin' mom said, "Really! That's wonderful! How will you do it?" Reactions from just about everyone else were to be far less enthusiastic, to say the least. But I could always count on my mother to understand that certain things were important to me. That's an unusual skill to have. So many parents spend their lives trying to mold their children to a pre-existing image of what they think happiness should be. My parents never did that to me. They always knew my life was my own.

"I'm not sure exactly what's involved, but I absolutely, positively know that's what I'm going to do with my life." I sat down on the edge of the bed and faced her expectantly.

"What about the languages?"

"Think about it, Mom. I'll be coming into contact with all sorts of people and maybe I'll be able to fly internationally. I'm sure there will be plenty of use for them."

"I don't think I've ever heard of a female airline pilot," she mused. "Are there any?"

"I don't know." I'd never given it any thought. "But if there aren't, there are about to be!"

"It sounds expensive. How will you pay for it?"

"I don't know," I said. "What would you do?"

"Well," she said, reaching for my hand, "it's probably a lot of money. Why don't you go get a real estate license and sell a few houses? That ought to bring in enough for a good start." It made sense. My mother was not an agent, but was a knowledge-able investor.

So I went and got my real estate license after taking a quickie weekend real estate course, and sold houses to a few of my college professors. My mom even helped me with the paperwork. With the commissions I earned I paid for my flight lessons. At the time, it was a perfect solution. I am profoundly grateful to my mother for suggesting this route.

I sometimes say to people that my biggest gift was knowing *exactly* what I wanted to do at a very young age. I appreciated that gift even more so in later years when I saw people all around me floundering, not knowing what they wanted from life, being passionate about nothing, wasting their lives watching meaningless sitcoms or just "hanging out" with no purpose, no intent and no direction, not really living but just existing with unfulfilling minimum or near-minimum wage jobs. I can't even imagine a desk job, trading dollars for hours. Trading dollars for doing something I remain passionate about is an entirely different matter.

Being an airline pilot is demanding, sometimes exhausting, sometimes even frustrating, with weather, mechanical and other problems to deal with, but to call it "work" would be a travesty as far as I'm concerned. Of course, I feel we deserve to be paid well for what we do, but that's simply a benefit. In his wonderful book *Catch Me If You Can* Frank Abagnale refers to working for an airline as "The Land of Milk and Honey." To this day, even with all the restrictions resulting from ugly world events, as far as I'm concerned it's still true.

Frank Abagnale, incidentally, is someone whom I practically idolized after I first read his book in the early 80s. I can practically hear the clucks of disapproval as I write this. I did not look up to him because he was one of the world's great con men—absolutely not. I've been conned myself here and there over the years and I've never been amused by it, and certainly I haven't admired those who perpetrated the cons. My admiration stemmed from the fact that of all the personality traits I value, I rank creativity right up there at the top.

When I first heard Mr. Abagnale had actually gotten away with impersonating a Pan Am pilot, I was as stunned as I'm sure most people were. But what was most surprising of all is how he went about it. The sheer ingeniousness of it was, and is, inspiring.

To this day I am grateful that I knew with complete and utter certainty that I was to be an airline pilot. My mental image was of a United Airlines airplane, that image certainly influenced by the New York crew who took such good care of me a few years before when I was flying home from Israel.

Since my career decision had struck me with such certainty, there was nothing left to do but go and make it happen. It was probably to my advantage that I had no foresight of the almost overwhelming struggle that lay ahead.

# CHAPTER 9

## Uuunnnnggghhh

After that first night in the cockpit, there was no way I could wait to start learning how to fly. The other class, the one I was most interested in, was Private Pilot Ground School, held for the very first time the next evening. I didn't even know what a "private pilot" was. I didn't have any preconceived notions about how to get where I was going—I simply had no idea whatsoever what was involved.

The instructor, John Curtin, was a tan, athletic-looking man with sun-bleached hair. He looked more like a surfer to me than a pilot. Although physically imposing, he was easy-going with a wonderful sense of humor—a trait common to the majority of pilots I've met.

The first night was mostly an introduction to aviation and I got my first real taste of what was involved—there was far more to learn than just the actual flying part.

When you learn to drive a car, it's mostly about getting the feel of the car. In learning to fly, there are corollary requirements. Pilots must learn navigation—both by instruments and by "dead-reckoning," which basically means measuring your course and distance from a known point, like a recognizable landmark.

There was meteorology, a subject I had never even considered. We also had to learn about FARs (Federal Aviation Regulations), what constituted visual versus instrument flight rules, fuel and oil consumption rates, weight and balance for the airplane, radio procedures, airport markings, how to make conversions concerning temperature and altitude when flight planning, and different categories of altitude and airspeed, like "density altitude" and "true airspeed." There were also endless acronyms to learn. The list seemed endless, but fascinating. I couldn't get enough of it.

We had to learn to use a flight computer—basically a circular slide rule—for temperature and altitude conversions. We had to learn to read Jeppesen charts, named for Elrey Jeppesen, a United Airlines pilot who had been an early barnstormer. Pilots and airlines worldwide use his charts, and the main terminal at Denver International Airport was named for him.

I felt that at the end of the course I would have some knowledge in at least a dozen different areas. It was the most interesting endeavor I'd ever undertaken. Languages were easy for me and certainly entertaining, but they were pretty one-dimensional. It was like breaking a code and trying to be accurate with pronunciation and grammar, but that was pretty much it.

Aviation was a whole new world opening up to me, right then and there during that first evening of Private Pilot Ground School. Of course, I really wanted to start learning to fly right away, and after class that first night I approached John. Again, I was the only female in the class of about twenty guys, one or two of whom I recognized from the Airport Management course.

"Um, I wanted to talk to you about flying. Are you busy?" I started moving to a chair in front of his desk.

He politely closed the folder from which he was reading and placed his hands on his desk. "Not at all. Have a seat."

"Thanks," I said, leaning forward toward him. "I'm going to be an airline  pilot, and I need to know how to go about doing it."

A smile played across his lips. "Yes, Meryl, everyone who gets their pilot's license wants to be a Pan Am 747 pilot."

I was dead serious and ignored the sarcasm. "Well, yes, that's pretty much what I have in mind. Pan Am would be nice," I waved my hand, "but I'll settle for any major airline. I have my eye on United as my first choice, but I'd certainly settle for Pan Am."

He laughed, a strong, good-natured laugh, amused by my presumption, but somehow knowing better than to argue with me. He certainly knew that I'd have to find out for myself that relatively few pilots with my aspirations ever made it to the top. "Well, you're in the right place for it."

"How does it work? What do I need to do?"

"First, you have to pass a written exam. Then you'll need forty hours of flight instruction and *then*, whenever you're ready, you'll have to take a check ride in an airplane with an FAA examiner. You'll also need a third-class medical. Get that squared away before you do anything else. It's required for student pilots. This class will get you up to speed to pass the written."

"Okay, what else?"

His eyes flickered with momentary surprise, but he continued on. "No doubt you know that flying is expensive. Your best bet is to join a flying club."

"What does that mean? Are you in one?"

"Yes, I am. It's a terrific club called Coastal Flyers, but it's hard to get in because they have really cheap rates and everyone wants those. Anyway, you buy stock when you join, so that you have part ownership of their airplanes."

My eyes widened. *Own a plane!* I nodded vigorously, encouraging him to tell me more. "Where do I sign up?"

"You can't, not right now. There's got to be an opening, plus I'm sure there's a waiting list. Always is."

I would not be deterred. "How much does it cost?"

"Well, it varies, but right now it's about $200 to join. Then, when you leave, you sell the stock—you always get a little profit out of that."

"Can't you put me on the list? I'll find a deposit—"

John held up his hand to stop me. He knew exactly where I was going. "I'll get you on the list, but don't hold your breath. Some people have waited months, or even years."

I must have looked crestfallen, because he suggested I get started with lessons. "In the meantime, we can set you up to take flight lessons over at Gillespie Field, in Santee. That's east of El Cajon. Can you get out there okay?"

"Yes, of course!"

"That's where Coastal Flyers keeps their planes and you may as well start there."

"There's a decent guy there at the FBO—that stands for Fixed Base Operator—at the base of the control tower. Ask for Chuck Harris. He's a good instructor and I'm sure he'll take you on. I'd do it myself but I'm just too busy."

I hadn't even realized that John was a flight instructor himself. "I'll go right over there tomorrow to get started!" I squeaked, barely able to contain my excitement. "Can I call him tonight? What's his number?"

"Why don't I give him a call and see what he can do. Remember, I said it's expensive."

"I'll find a way to earn the money. But I've *got* to fly."

The next morning I went and got my third-class physical taken care of. I also went and got my FCC (Federal Communications Commission) license, which John had told me I'd need before I could talk on the radio. No problem there—I paid my $25 and it was mine.

By that afternoon I was standing in a hangar over at Gillespie Field. Chuck Harris was a stocky, middle-aged man who looked like he'd taken one-too-many annoying people on jaunts to golf courses up at Pebble Beach or over in Palm Springs. He practically heaved an audible sigh of resignation when he saw me approaching, my face beaming and hand outstretched.

"Meryl Getline, Mr. Harris. Nice to meet you."

"All right, then," he shook my hand perfunctorily. "You ready to fly?"

"You bet I am!"

"Let me see your physical. You have it, right?"

"Yep! Just got it!"

"Have you passed your written yet?"

"No, not yet, but I will." I didn't mention I'd had exactly two hours of ground school less than twenty-four hours before. I wasn't sure exactly what John had told him.

"What's your goal? Just a private? Do you even want your license or are you just doing this for fun?"

"I'm gong to be an airline pilot," I announced.

"Oh, God," he said with some irritation. "Not another one. Listen, I'll take you up now, but I want that written passed before you blow too much money on flight lessons. A lot of people get started, never get their written passed, and get mad because I didn't make a big enough deal of it."

"Understood," I said. "I'll get it passed as soon as I can."

"Sure," he responded unenthusiastically.

This was not starting off well at all. "Listen," I said, "airline pilots get to be airline pilots some way. Why do you think I can't do it?"

"First of all," he held up his index finger, "you're a girl. Strike One. Second of all, even if you were a highly qualified guy, you'd never get hired because all the airlines have laid off thousands of pilots. It'll be years before they get called back, if they get called back at all. Strike Two." The middle finger joined the index. "Third, you can't train to be an airline pilot flying little airplanes around. They want 'heavy time'. Strike Three. Is that enough for you?"

"What exactly does that mean?" I asked. "What's 'heavy time'?"

"It's real airplane time, big airplane time."

"Okay," I said. "Where do you get it?"

"Most airline guys come straight out of the Air Force or Navy. And before you say it—forget it. They don't let women fly in the military. You'll never get on with an airline. Do you still want to go up, now that you know you'll never make it?" (In fact, American Airlines did hire its first woman, Bonnie Tiburzi, on March 15, 1973, the same month I began flying lessons. Bonnie was the first woman to be hired by any of the major airlines. I did not learn of it for years, however, mainly because the flow of information was not as widespread as it is today. Unfortunately, she was furloughed at the end of December that same year and did not get called back for over two years.)

Without another word, Chuck turned on his heel and headed out to the tarmac. I didn't need an invitation to follow him. Of course I still wanted to go. His words made a deep impression on me, but not the impression he meant to make. He made me realize for the first time that this was going to be a serious uphill battle for all the reasons he'd said, and then some, but his negative attitude had exactly the opposite effect that I'm sure he intended; it strengthened, even cemented, my resolve. I didn't care what he thought. I had my goal and it was my job to ensure I made it happen. Failure was not an option.

We approached a Cessna-150, a very small, high-wing plane. Frank Knight's airplane had been a low-wing plane. You had to step on the wing to enter Frank's plane, but in the Cessna you just got in similar to getting into a car, only the seat was slightly higher.

Chuck stopped in front of the plane and held his hands up in front of him, as if he was about to push the plane away. "Now, I'm gonna show you this step-by-step. First you do a walkaround, check everything out and make sure it looks right. 'Course, you won't know what looks right and what doesn't first off, but you will."

He sauntered around the plane, pointing at various parts. "Okay, then, let's get in. You're on the left." This was my first time in the left seat, and I was surprised. That's the pilot-in-command seat, but it's also where students sit. Frank had sat in the left seat on our flight the night before.

As I scrambled into the cockpit I asked, "Where're we headed?"

He buckled in. "Up to Oceanside. We'll do a touch-and-go, that's what you call—"

"—landing and taking off again without stopping," I proudly finished the sentence for him.

One corner of his mouth started to smile. "Yeah, that's right."

After more pointing, this time at the instruments, we got clearance and headed for the runway.

The sun was still bright in the sky, and everything was clear. We bumped along, gathering speed, and finally lifted off the ground. It felt slower than it had at night, but was just as exciting.

Until I started getting nauseous. We'd hadn't even reached our final altitude when I started feeling sick. *Oh, no!* Chuck was pointing out some sights and talking about gaining altitude, and other relevant flying information, but I was too preoccupied with fighting the increasing urge to throw up.

Though I didn't know Chuck well enough to say for sure, I had a strong suspicion that he'd rather toss me out of the plane than let me throw up in it. *I* didn't want to throw up. How in the world could this be happening? I'd found my life's calling and it was making me sick. Again.

Chuck must have looked over at me because he asked if I was all right. "You look like a green olive."

I shot him a horrified look—not because I was afraid of how I looked, but because the words "green olive" almost put me out cold. If I spent one more second imagining one of those things—and, *oh, God, no* with pimentos!—I would have been a goner. My eyelids fluttered, and I swallowed hard.

"Here, kid," he snapped his fingers at me. "Meryl, come on try the controls. You steer, and that'll get your mind onto something else."

I made a feeble attempt, all the while cursing my bad fortune. But it was no use. Chuck reached over, patting my face. "You all right there, Meryl? Not gonna heave on me, are you?"

"Uuuunnnggghhhh."

Chuck took that as a maybe. "I'm gonna have to head back here, Meryl."

"Nnngghaaaaa!"

"I know, I know. It's a disappointment. I'm, uh, I'm disappointed too. Yes, I sure am."

I then found out what can happen if you suppress the need to throw up long enough. I passed out, but only for a few seconds before I was back to my conscious, fully nauseated, highly green self.

I couldn't believe it. After only five minutes in the air, Chuck was taking us back. I was now the color of lime sherbet and incoherent to boot.

Back at Gillespie, Chuck helped me out of the plane. Once he realized I was clear of the plane, he became downright paternal, and practically carried me to the bathroom. I emerged a good twenty minutes later, after many splashes of cold water, a fully recovered Meryl. Chuck was waiting for me in his office.

"I'm ready to go back up."

He looked up at me from his desk, both of his chins completely melded with his neck. After a big sigh he said, "Meryl, not only no, but *hell* no. I'm sorry, but I won't be able to give you any more lessons. Flying is not for you. It's better you know now than later so you can start thinking of something else. Some people just aren't cut out for this. You probably have an imbalance in your inner ear or something. And the whole airline thing just isn't going to happen. It isn't possible for a girl. You need to go find something else you can do."

"No! It's a fluke. I'm sure of it..." My voice trailed off. I was lying through my teeth. I knew very well that almost every time I'd flown before I'd gotten airsick if I wasn't sick already with a cold or something else. Whenever I'd tried multiple turns in ballet or skating, or a series of tumbles in gymnastics class, I had gotten dizzy beyond what was considered normal. My mother had a huge tendency toward motion sickness. Maybe I inherited it from her. But wait! "I go sailing with my dad and brothers all the time, and I've never, ever gotten seasick."

Chuck looked at me with pity and shook his head. "Sorry, Meryl."

"I'll build up an immunity."

"I won't charge you for the lesson, such as it was," he patted the air in my general direction, trying to assuage my feelings. I had the distinct impression this was the sort of man who wouldn't know what to do with little girls who cried or women who behaved petulantly.

"If you're so set on planes, I'm sure you could go into management or become an air traffic controller. By the time you're ready, they might be letting women do some of that."

I realized that Chuck was a lost cause, so I thanked him and went back to Montgomery Field. It was early evening, and John Curtin was getting ready for class. I found him at the chalkboard making notes.

I slumped down in a chair and heaved a big, Scarlett O'Hara-esque sigh.

John turned around. "Hey, Meryl, did you get a lesson in? What did you think of Chuck?"

I rolled my eyes. "Airsick. Chuck wouldn't keep the plane up. I think he thought I was going to heave all over."

His eyes softened. "Well, that's just a shame."

"And I passed out."

"Oh."

We were silent for a moment. I hadn't the energy to hold up both ends of the conversation just then. John turned back to the board and started writing. Then, abruptly, he stopped. "Hey, Meryl, didn't you say you flew with Frank Knight after class the other night?"

"Yeah."

"And no airsickness?"

"Nope. Nothing."

"When have you got sick before this?"

"Commercial flights."

"All of them?"

"No. On some I was fine. Some I was sick already with a cold or flu or something."

"Well, then, you're not always airsick, are you," he said matter-of-factly.

I straightened up in my chair. "You're right."

"So we just have to figure out what's making you sick."

My smile was bigger than any airsickness I'd ever felt. John might not have had a lot to say, but when he did say something, it was meaningful. And almost better still, he wasn't telling me to go find another career.

"Okay, so you flew with Frank at night."

"Yes."

"What about the flights when you were sick, day or night?"

I thought a moment, then said, "Day. I'm almost positive they were all day. I'm pretty much a night person all the way around." I inherited that trait from my mother, too.

"Can you stay after class? Let's go back out to Gillespie and I'll take you up tonight. We'll see what happens with another night flight."

I couldn't believe it! I was going back up that night!

After class we headed back over to Gillespie, and John took me up for about two hours. He gave me an actual flight lesson, my first logged flight in my brand new Pilot's Logbook. Chuck hadn't logged our five-minute "trauma-ride," as I later dubbed it, and I was just as glad he didn't.

John started with the preflight walkaround, what to check for, a basic briefing on all the primary instruments, what to say on the radio. Everything was explained, from start to finish.

To this day I generally prefer night flying, but I would slowly but surely get over the daytime airsickness. That night I felt fine, on top of the world. I didn't feel even the slightest queasiness. Even though I've never really found a satisfactory answer, we did establish that my airsickness was confined to daylight hours. At night I was just fine. Building up immunity was a slow and painful process, but I eventually did.

After we landed and taxied back to park, we sat talking in the plane.

"What do you say we give nights a try for awhile?" John asked.

"Really?!" I couldn't believe my good luck. "But how?"

"Me."

"You're kidding! You'll take me as a student?"

"Yup. And that's not all. Apparently, you've got some luck."

"What? What?" I was practically jumping up and down in my seat.

"Coastal Flyers has an opening."

"Wha—Really? How? Wait! Don't answer that. How come you didn't tell me before we went up?" I practically shouted.

"I had to make sure you were going to survive. Because if you'd gotten sick again, I was going to tell you to forget the whole thing. And even if you didn't forget it, I sure as hell wouldn't have wanted to be your instructor." He broke into a big grin, and so did I. Then he became somber. "You know girls aren't allowed to be airline pilots, right?"

"So I've heard. Chuck told me—thoroughly."

"I'll get you your ratings, but you'll never fly commercially. I don't think anyone will hire a girl."

"They won't be hiring a girl," I said defiantly. "They'll be hiring a pilot. I know what I want and nobody's going to tell me I can't fly because I'm a girl. That's just silly." Of course, it would prove to be infinitely more difficult than I initially thought.

We sat in silence for a moment, and then it dawned on me. I turned back to John. "How in the world did an opening in Coastal Flyers come up so quickly?" I asked suspiciously. "What about that long waiting list?"

John said with a knowing grin, "That waiting list was long for ages, and people just stopped adding their names." He shrugged. "I guess the list shrank. The people ahead of you gave up and went somewhere else."

I love people who give up. I have no respect for them, of course —allowing for unavoidable circumstances— but I still love them. They make it so much easier for the rest of us.

And so I started down the road—the impossibly long road—toward my ultimate goal of being a captain for United Airlines.

## CHAPTER 10

# Wanted: Dolphin Rider

Growing up I'd always had jobs, or started little businesses to earn travel money. For most of my college years, however, I'd stuck with academics, lived at home, and saved whatever money I happened into.

One thing I never did, however, when it came to jobs, was the ordinary. I couldn't, like so many college kids I knew, wait tables or be someone's nanny. I tried something like that once or twice and discovered I was just terrible at it and lasted only a couple of weeks. I needed something involving at least a little fun.

Once a college friend helped me get a job serving food to sailors in the galley at one of the Naval facilities in San Diego. My boss hit on me, and after just a few weeks I was ready to quit anyway. It just wasn't in me to do something so unimaginative for very long.

The sailors I served were seemingly without humor, but were actually very responsive when I said something even remotely funny or witty. It was then I started to appreciate the fact that so many people's lives were lived with such little enjoyment or humor that even the slightest remark from me would elicit smiles. As I was slopping corned beef hash onto some sailor's tray, I'd say something like, "Will Monsieur be ordering the Chateau Briande with sauce Bernaise, or perhaps Monsieur would prefer the Glazed Hummingbirds' Tongues with a lovely Pilaf?" It was so easy to get a laugh out of them, that I did feel some regret when I left—but not that much. I knew I had to do better.

The real estate thing was lucrative, but the money was dependent upon sales, and they were rather few and far between. As a matter of fact, the only houses I ever sold were to some of my hapless college professors, God love' em. What I did do, however, was examine whatever talent or skill I had, and figure out a way to make money with it.

One thing I'd always loved to do was swim. So it was a natural for me to apply for a job at Sea World. They'd run an ad looking for girls with long hair who were strong but elegant swimmers and didn't mind squeezing into a rubber fin. There was a show at Charlie Tuna's Underwater Theater in which girls dressed up as mermaids and swam with dolphins.

I walked to the front gate of Sea World, explaining I was there for a job. They pointed me toward a small booth.

"Good morning," I said to the young guy in the booth. "I'm here for a job interview."

"Hello," he said, with a stunning lack of enthusiasm. "Have you ever worked one before?

"Worked one what?" I asked, mystified.

"A snack bar, of course," he said.

"No, do you have to have snack bar experience to ride dolphins?"

"Look, are you here for dolphins or burgers?"

"Dolphins. Swimming with, not eating."

He looked at me blandly. "Just go over to the Underwater Theater, the blue building, and let them know you're here."

"Thanks!" I said. "Wish me luck!"

There was a surprising number of mermaid-wannabes already standing about, and more came in after me. While standing in line to fill out an application—the right line this time—some girls behind me expressed concern about swimming with dolphins, while another was excited about the opportunity to "commune with nature."

I turned to her and said, "You realize you're putting on a rubber fin, right? And then getting into a man-made tank with tamed dolphins that perform tricks?" She ignored me.

The application consisted of the basics: name, sex, address and phone number. Then there were the more interesting questions, such as whether or not you'd feel constricted in a rubber body suit, whether or not you had any allergies to rubber, and whether or not you'd be willing to take basic water-safety training. I'd had a "junior lifeguard" certification for years and felt very at home in the water. I didn't have a problem with any of the requirements.

The dolphins, it turned out, were all business. They may be smiling all the time, but inside, they just want to get the job done, have some fish, and be left alone. I suppose I'd feel the same way, too, if I had to be cute and jump through hoops on command. Though I suppose we humans devise enough absurd things for us to do ourselves—the ridiculousness of the mermaid gig was not lost on me—there's something perverse about non-human animal tricks.

Our interviewer, the dolphins' trainer, didn't ask us to put on any fins. Instead, after we filled out the application we were herded into a locker room to change into bathing suits. Then we were led, five at a time, to a big tank, and told to jump in and get acclimated to the temperature, which was rather cool. It didn't bother me a bit. Growing up in San Diego with Meredith (my pet mallard) I went swimming year-round in water as cold as fifty degrees. This water was about sixty-five degrees or so.

We lined up around the edge of the tank and the trainers brought in three dolphins. With a simple command, one of the dolphins swam up to us and just sort of hung out. "Okay, the first brunette there," the trainer said, pointing to me and, sounding about as enthusiastic as a monotone voice can be, said, "grab on to the dorsal fin and hold on. The dolphin will take you around the tank. Just hang on until I tell you to let go, okay?"

I nodded, and reached for the fin. The dolphin started to dart off before I was ready, and I lost my grasp. But immediately, the dolphin slowed down, allowing me to regain my hold. *Amateur!* I imagined him (or her) thinking. The ride was fast and actually a lot of fun.

After three turns about the tank, the trainer barked an order to my dolphin, which then deposited me, without fanfare, back at my starting point. Then the dolphin moved on to some of the more timid girls there. The first girl chickened out and bolted out of the tank as fast as she could, while another one gasped audibly all the way around the pool. The trainer threw her out after just one turn. If the dolphin thought I was an amateur, he must have thought she was a most insubstantial human. How degrading it must be to be smarter than your handler!

Now it was Communing-With-Nature's turn. Going for something like a cross between Esther Williams and a Rockette, she turned on an enormous smile and waved all the way around the tank—three times! To her credit, she never once faltered.

After the last in our group went, the trainer brought in a few more girls to replace the one who'd fled and the other he'd kicked out. The dolphins performed a few more perfunctory routines with us, and then we were dismissed. "We'll call you," the trainer said. Apparently this was his day job until Hollywood called him.

A few days later, I actually did get a call from Sea World asking me to come back for another round of auditions, this time in the fin suit. But when they asked if I could commit to thirty hours, six days a week, including both training and performances, I had to decline. Going to class during the day and flying at night meant I'd need to have a more flexible schedule. Actually, I'm not sure when I thought I was going to find time to do this in the first place, but it looked like fun. I was disappointed it didn't work out, but at least I'd had the opportunity to swim with a dolphin.

## CHAPTER 11

## Whose Learjet Is This, Anyway?

The very evening of the audition I had ground school again. John asked to see me after class. After everyone had filed out, he motioned for me to come up to the front of the class where he was erasing the board. "Meryl," he said seriously, "we have to discuss costs."

"Oh!" I slapped my forehead. "John, I am so sorry. I was so excited to fly I completely forgot to ask you about it."

"Now, normally you'd be paying $30 an hour, wet, but being a member of the club means you pay only $7. It's really an incredible deal." Then he broke into a smile. So did I.

"I can do that. What does 'wet' mean?"

John explained that it meant the rate included fuel, which wasn't always the case. He also explained that although Coastal Flyers had a Cessna-150, the same type of two-seater I'd gone up in with Chuck Harris, it was actually slightly cheaper to rent one of the two Cessna-172's, which were four-seaters. To me at that stage it was the difference between a "little" plane and a "big" plane. The rate was calculated at $7 per hour for the smaller Cessna-150, and $7.50 for the larger Cessna-172, but the Cessna-150 was on "Hobbs" time, meaning there was a meter (Hobbsmeter) which racked up time by the minute.

The Cessna-172's, on the other hand, used "Tach" (tachometer) time. Although the rate was a little higher, it racked up time according to how fast the engine was turning. All the time spent taxiing or descending was charged at a very low rate, making the average hourly rate only about $6.90 per hour. That was incredibly cheap, even in the early 70's, and that is why I learned to appreciate even more whatever fluke of timing allowed me admittance into this extraordinary flight club.

"What about your rate, John? You charge separately, right?"

He shook his head. "No rate. I'll see you through all your ratings. You buy me dinner once in awhile and we'll call it even."

"What? John, Why would you do that? I do appreciate it, but I can't not pay you. That's not right."

"Meryl, everyone should have a leg up now and then. Believe me, if you're serious about angling for a career as a pilot, this will likely be the last favor you see. Take advantage of it."

I took a deep breath and held out my hand. "Deal." We shook. "You won't regret this, John. I don't care what anybody says, I'm going to make it to the majors and I'll have you to thank."

We stood there for a moment, smiling somewhat awkwardly. "So, uh, are we going to fly tonight?"

He laughed a deep, hearty laugh, and said, "Meryl, you're something else." Then he added waving me along, "Come on, let's go. But after tonight, there's some required reading for you to do. I won't even consider taking on a student who hasn't read Wolfgang Langewiesche's *Stick and Rudder*. I'll loan you my copy, but every pilot should read it and own it. It was published in the 40's, but it's as worthwhile today as it was then. You should also read *Weather Flying* by Robert Buck and *Instrument Flying* by Robert Taylor."

I read all of these as fast as I could and found all of them invaluable. I loved to read, and went to the library to see what else there was about aviation in general and being an airline pilot in particular. All the materials I could find about airline pilots were directed to men, of course, saying such helpful things as how important it would be to consider a stint in the Air Force or Navy, since the most desirable pilots from the airlines' point of view were military pilots. That didn't do me any good at all.

One book caught my eye. It was called *She'll Never Get Off The Ground*, by Robert J. Serling. I read the flap of the book and I couldn't believe it! Here was a book published two years prior, in 1971, about a fictional female airline pilot. There certainly weren't any female airline pilots in 1971 and I couldn't understand why it would occur to anyone to write this book. It was like reading about my own future, and was both eerie and inspiring.

I proceeded to read it as fast as I could and determined I just *had* to speak with the author. Using just the information on the flap of the book, I tracked down the author at his home in Bethesda, Maryland, and told him that *I* wanted to be the first female airline pilot. When I asked him *why* he would write a book about the first female airline pilot when there weren't any yet, his response was simply, "I thought it'd make a good story." It certainly did.

I'm not sure I've ever met anyone who isn't familiar with Rod Serling's "The Twilight Zone". Rod was Robert's younger brother, and we talked about him, too, when I met with Robert Serling in Los Angeles, just before he was to appear on a television talk show. He talked about the production of the episode with the "gremlin" out on the wing of an airliner in flight. "Twilight Zone" fans will remember that one. I went on to read every one of Robert Serling's books, of which there are many, both fiction and non-fiction.

When we got to Gillespie Field, John went straight over to where the planes were parked, and I was practically hopping along beside him in excitement. "Which planes are ours?" I asked breathlessly. I was like a kid in a candy store who was already well into a sugar-high.

There was a whole row of airplanes belonging to Coastal Flyers: A Cessna-150, two Cessna-172's and a few Cessna-182's, which are slightly more sophisticated aircraft. I couldn't believe so many airplanes were in. A lot of Coastal Flyer members flew only for pleasure, and not that often.

John stopped in front of one of the planes. "This is ours tonight. 8178 Lima." The "L" in the registration number was pronounced using the phonetic alphabet, something else I'd need to learn. It was blue, it was beautiful, and, for the moment, it was mine!

We did our walkaround with flashlights, and then got in. John quizzed me on start-up procedures from my previous flight with him and then had me call for taxi instructions, dictating exactly what to say.

Up in the air, it was like a dream. We were higher than I'd been in Knight's Cherokee, and though there were two of us, the solitude felt more profound, with far less conversation than there had been with Frank Knight. John's instructions were precise and economical, which allowed me to focus on what I was doing. Once we reached altitude, I took the controls for the first time. It was as natural as breathing.

After that night I pretty much lived at Gillespie Field. Because of the distance between home in Point Loma, school at San Diego State, and the airport even farther east in Santee, it made more sense for me to sleep where I flew and then get up the next morning and go to school. I kept my sleeping bag with me and spent many nights under the wing of "my" plane.

My routine was fairly simple: I took flying lessons most weekdays from eleven at night to three in the morning, camped out next to 8178L and then went to school later that morning where I showered and went to class. More often than not, I went back to the field after classes to hang out in the coffee shop and try to meet other pilots, or went up to the control tower to learn as much about ATC (air traffic control) procedures as I could.

Before long, I'd spent so much time at the airport that people called me by my plane's tail number instead of my name. I loved it when people addressed me as "78 Lima."

After a few weeks of camping out by my airplane, the Tower Chief at Gillespie Field, Ed Gray, learned I was sleeping under the wing of my plane. One night, before John and I took off, another pilot came over and said Ed wanted me to come up. I headed over to the tower. "Hey, Ed. I heard you were looking for me?"

"Hey there, Meryl." Ed was a clean-cut, lean guy with whom I'd had only the briefest of conversations. "I hear you've been spending a lot of nights out here."

*Uh-oh, I'm in trouble.* There's probably something illegal about it. "Oh, yeah," I stammered, shifting my weight from foot to foot. "You know, I just—John's taking me up nights, because of school and everything, and sometimes I just stay when it's so late."

"Here." He handed me a key. "It's the key to the tower. Use the lounge downstairs, with the couch. It's a little safer than out with the planes. If you get here after we close, just let yourself in."

I pocketed the key to the tower. "Thanks, Ed, really. That's just great." I couldn't believe it.

"Don't mention it," he smiled. "*Really*, don't mention it. Before you know it, everybody'll want a key."

"My lips are sealed." And with that, my new address became The Tower at Gillespie Field.

Years later, entirely by coincidence, my father was returning from a business trip and wound up sitting next to Ed Gray on the flight home. They struck up a conversation, and each man learned who the other was. Ed admitted he knew only my first name. As far as he was concerned, my last name was 8178L.

Spending all my time at the airport certainly had its advantages. As different airplanes would arrive, I'd seek out their owners and sometimes would be invited up to go flying.

One day, when I arrived at the airport on a Saturday morning, I saw my first corporate jet, a stunning, sleek, exquisite thing that someone told me was a Learjet. It was all locked up, but I pressed my face against the windows trying to see inside. Someone called to me that the owner was in the coffee shop having breakfast.

I pretty much knew all the regulars, and it wasn't difficult to spot the guys flying the Lear, sitting at a table, eating breakfast. I approached the table and said, "I don't want to interrupt your breakfast, but does that Learjet belong to you guys?"

The man closest to me answered, "It's mine, why?"

"Because it's the most gorgeous airplane I've ever seen. After you're done eating, could you possible show me the cockpit?"

"Tell you what, we can do better than that. Would you like to go up? What's your interest, anyway?"

"I'm taking flight lessons," and yes, yes, *yes* I wanted to go up!

"Well, have a seat with us and drink some coffee or something while you tell us all about yourself. I've never met a woman pilot. What's your name?"

"Meryl," I said.

"Meryl, I'm Bill. This is Jack, Tom, and Mike. We're here just for a half-day or so, but we'll be happy to take you out for a spin."

The one introduced as Tom said, "Meryl, it's nice to meet you. Bill is being too modest. If you want to compliment the jet, you came to the right place. This is Bill Lear. As in Learjet."

I couldn't believe it! As they finished breakfast, I pretty much sat there and gawked, and afterward they showed me the beautiful jet and took me for a ride, Bill Lear in the left seat and me in the right. We flew over to Lindbergh Field where we shot a couple of touch-and-goes, and then came back.

Later that evening when it was time for my lesson with John, I told him what had happened. The Lear was gone by then, and he was stunned at my news.

"Woman, I cannot *believe* your luck sometimes," he was to say over and over for the next several months.

I've had many occasions to fly Learjets since then, and they're always exciting to fly, but no flight could match the one I shared with its inventor, Mr. Bill Lear.

## CHAPTER 12

## Oh, Solo Meryl

My next lesson was my first solo flight. "You ready?" John asked.

"I've *been* ready!" I said with excitement.

"All right, then. I'll be observing from the tower." He patted me on the shoulder. "You know what to do."

I did. There was take-off, then three touch-and-goes, and then a final landing. I was ready and felt great. By then, my daytime airsickness was pretty well under control and my first solo flight was at about eleven in the morning on a beautiful, clear day.

Taxiing out to the runway, I couldn't help smiling. The first time I'd gotten into a plane to become a pilot I'd been overwhelmed by the number and diversity of instruments. Now I was flying solo and feeling almost like an old pro. I radioed the control tower for take-off clearance. And I was off!

Once I had my first solo ride I think I spent more time in the air than on the ground. I went all over, as far east as Blythe, on the border of California and Arizona; as far north as Santa Barbara and all over the greater San Diego area. The flying rate was so cheap that, as it turned out, selling the occasional house was enough to finance all the required hours. If I'd had to take a "real" job, I couldn't have managed enough time to get my flight ratings as quickly as I did. I was eternally grateful to my mother for her suggesting I get that real estate license.

Within the month I took and passed my written test for my Private Pilot license. I got the requisite forty hours for the Private Pilot rating as quickly as I possibly could. John arranged for an FAA inspector to come out for my check ride. Glen Hesler was an ex-Air Force colonel, very friendly and very anxious to put me at ease. "Don't worry about anything, Meryl, just fly your airplane and pretend I'm not even here. We'll go have ourselves a nice flight, and when we come back I'll sign you off!"

He acted like there was no point in even discussing the possibility of failure, and I appreciated his positive and comforting attitude.

I did the walkaround, and then John wished me luck as Glen and I boarded the plane. I radioed ground control to get permission for taxi to the runway. Finally, I contacted the control tower for clearance to take-off.

"Cleared for take-off," the tower controller responded, then added, "John's standing right here with us. He says 'good luck,' and that goes for all of us."

Glen smiled and said, "Well, you seem mighty popular. It's great you have so many people up there wishing you luck and wanting to see you get your license."

We took off and I just told myself to relax. *People did this all the time. I knew exactly what I was doing and I wasn't just going to pass, I was going to do the best check ride in the history of the world.*

Well, I don't know about that, but I was very happy with my performance. John and I had had contests, seeing who could make the softest touchdown, and sometimes I beat him. If nothing else, I wanted the three requisite landings to be as perfect as possible, and they were. The landings were so smooth, in fact, that when we touched down each time, I heard Glen murmur, "Sweet," under his breath.

After the last landing, Glen took the radio and said to the tower, "Congratulate her, boys! She just got her license!"

John took the tower radio and said, "Congratulations, Meryl! We all knew you could do it! I'll see you and Glen at the base of the tower." He was beaming when we met him outside the tower, and gave me a big hug. "Nicely done. So who's going to be your first passenger?"

I smiled to myself. My mother was not keen on flying. In fact, I was virtually certain I'd inherited my airsickness from her. No one in my family was enamored of flying the way I was, not even my father. Nevertheless, my mother had told me she wanted to be my first official passenger.

I rushed home to tell her in person that I had passed. She was waiting for me in the living room, decked out in sneakers and sweat pants.

"I'm ready," she announced as I came in. Somehow she knew, as she always did, that she'd be going up with me.

"I did it!" I gave her a big hug.

"Of course you did," she hugged me back. "Now, take me flying."

"But Mom, are you sure? You don't have to do this."

"Nonsense. I want to be your first passenger. Come on, Meryl, let's go! You may as well start building some hours!"

Aside from the fact that I was terribly proud to fly my mother, I did need hours. John had sat down and mapped out a course for acquiring the different pilot ratings, to be accomplished as quickly as possible. First was the Private Pilot, then the Commercial, Instrument, Multi-Engine, Certified Flight Instructor and Certified Flight Instructor-Instruments.

Somewhere along the way I decided, what the heck, and threw in a Ground Instructor and Instrument Ground Instructor's rating. I remember taking several written exams in one week. The Airline Transport Rating—the Big Kahuna for me—would unfortunately have to wait. I wasn't yet old enough—you had to be twenty-three and I was just twenty—and fifteen hundred hours of flight time were required. That would take awhile and I couldn't possibly afford to pay for all that time. But first things first. And in this case, it was my first passenger. What a thrill it was for me to take my mom flying.

Though her face was taught and body rigid, she smiled at me in encouragement. I reached over and patted her leg. We headed out to the runway where I requested take-off clearance from the control tower. "Mom, are you sure you're okay? We don't have to do this."

"Don't be silly," she grimaced. "I wouldn't miss this for the world."

"Thanks, Mom. I promise to make it smooth."

We took off and I kept my promise. From the beginning, I have felt compelled to keep things as smooth as possible. With my mother on board, this was an imperative, as I knew her own tendency toward airsickness was as bad as mine had been.

To her credit, my mother did not close her eyes on take-off, and even managed to look about when I pointed out certain landmarks. After only a few minutes in the air, she began pointing out the window herself. It became a tour of sorts, me dividing my time between explaining to her what I was doing, where we were, what there was to see. I kept talking, pausing only to allow her to appreciate some sight or other.

"Can we fly over the house? Let's see, where would it be in relation to where we are now," she said to herself, and began twisting about to get a look.

"Hang on, let me change direction."

"Oh, Meryl, look!" The stretch of coastline spread out before us, with a clear view of the greater San Diego area, all the way to the mountains in the east. "Isn't this lovely? You know, I've never seen all this before. It's just beautiful."

I smiled, pleased to make my mother comfortable and share with her the love I had found. "You made all this happen for me, Mom. Thank you."

"No, Sweetheart, *you* made this happen." She laughed quietly. "You were so young. 'I have to fly, I have to fly.' If I'd only known!"

By the time we landed, my mother was as relaxed as can be, chatting away about this and that. It was an unforgettable flight for both of us.

It was easy to log hours—including cross-country time— for my commercial rating. Of course, I took my Dad up, and word got out at school that I had a pilot's license. Before long I was taking friends to all sorts of places, like Oceanside, Long Beach, Palm Springs, where we'd swim in any one of a number of hotels' pools, and the Salton Sea, where we would land at a strip right by the water and swim. My friends would chip in their share of the cost for the airplane, which kept the expense minimal for me.

John remained my instructor throughout the various ratings. He had told me that the Instrument Rating was the most difficult and most complex to obtain, but thanks to him, it was actually one of the easiest ratings for me. This is because, from day one with John, I didn't even realize there was any other way to fly than to use instruments. Many pilots who fly for pleasure fly visually, with only some reference to instruments for navigation. Instrument pilots learn to fly under a "hood," a plastic device you put over your head so you can't peek outside for visual reference.

Developing a good "scan" is of paramount importance when learning to fly on instruments. Fixating on a single instrument can spell trouble as other aspects of the flight could get out of control. Let's say you're fixating on your altimeter, trying to keep your airplane perfectly level, but if you don't keep that scan going, looking at each instrument in turn for just a second or two, suddenly you're off course, having neglected to keep an eye on your artificial horizon, never noticing that you were turning. You have to force yourself to keep your gaze moving. And when you're "visual," you have to "keep your head on a swivel," as John would say, while you kept an eye out for other air traffic.

There was a saying while flying under the hood that "one peek is worth a thousand scans." Sometimes John would have me look outside to reconcile the visual aspect with what I was seeing inside on the instrument panel.

One day, Glen Hesler, the examiner for all my ratings except the Airline Transport, which was to come much later, offered to fly with me for free all day among some of the busiest airports in the Los Angeles area. We flew to Long Beach, Orange County, Van Nuys, Burbank and Hawthorne. At each airport we would come to a full stop and taxi clear of the runway, and ask for an instrument clearance to the next stop. Pilots often had kneepads upon which to write clearances, but Glen's whole point was that he wanted me to listen carefully, and to be able to get the clearances correct without writing anything down. That was a tough one, as the clearances were complicated and I had never flown into any of these airports, but he was right there to back me up. And when I stumbled reading back the clearance to the controller, he would take over and do it for me.

We flew out to Catalina Island just off the Los Angeles coastline for lunch, having the requisite buffalo burgers that were the specialty out there, and then flew back and did some more practice instrument flights, getting clearance after clearance in quick succession.

That single day with Glen was worth years of experience in instrument flying, and it was so much fun being in that complex, busy, fast environment. I felt I was experiencing the "real thing" as opposed to flying around to the various small airports in San Diego. When I asked Glen why he would take his valuable time doing this, not even charging me (although he let me buy lunch when I insisted), his response was, "Because I want you to make it, that's why. I want you to be so good, so experienced and so proficient, they can't turn you down. That's why."

It was unnecessary to ask him who "they" were. He knew what my plans were and often told me, unlike so many others, that he firmly believed I'd achieve my goal.

People like Glen Hesler, John Curtin, Mr. Leon (during the "language years") a few other colorful characters that were to come into my life a little later, and, of course, my parents, were steadfast in their encouragement. Were it not for them, the story of how I got to where I am today might have taken an even more circuitous route. As it was, my next stop on the way to becoming a commercial airline pilot for United was Army boot camp. And may God help the U.S. Army!

## CHAPTER 13

# Boot Camp

"Dad, how do guys get to be airline pilots?" I'd asked soon after my realization that I was going to become an airline pilot. My father was in his usual chair, reading his usual paper, with me standing before him. Some things never change.

From behind his newspaper came the answer, "You gotta be in the Air Force."

"Is that the only way?" I asked

"Only way that I know of," he said. "I don't know where else you'd get the kind of time the airlines want." The paper rattled.

I did what I always do. I tracked down the person in charge, in this case a General at the Air Force Academy in Colorado Springs. I called the Academy, got put through to him, and said, "Hello, my name is Meryl Getline. I'm calling from San Diego. I'd like to know how to go about becoming an Air Force pilot."

"Honey," he said, his voice dripping with an ugly sweetness. "Ain't gonna happen."

"Why not?" I asked. "I'm a pilot now. What's the big deal?"

He dropped the fake sweetness. "The 'big deal,' as you put it, is that the Air Force is on combat status when it comes to flying. Women are not allowed on combat status."

"Not everything you guys fly is combat, though, is it?"

"Technically, yes. It doesn't matter if it's a flight from Moline to Peoria, it's all categorized under the same thing: combat status, and women are not allowed."

"But that has to change!" I cried. "I want to be an airline pilot. How am I supposed to get the flight time I need when all the guys are pretty much coming out of the Air Force?"

"Not my problem. You'll never fly for the Air Force and you'll certainly never fly for the airlines. Even if you got the time, they'd never hire a woman. In any case, those are the rules and it'll be at least twenty years before they'll let women into the Air Force to fly. Even then it would be too soon. Hell will freeze over before they're gonna let gals fly." And he hung up.

I would have liked to remind him of women like Jaqueline Cochran, who held more speed, distance, and altitude records than any other pilot—male or female—and the WASPS, those heroic women who risked their lives as pilots in World War II. But there seemed little point. As it turned out, the Air Force would change its rules just two years later, in 1976, and begin admitting women to flight school, but by then it would already be too late for me.

*Well, that was rude,* I thought as I called the Navy, where I got an only slightly less hostile response. They, in fact, had recently begun accepting women into their program, but there were no openings at all and none expected for the next couple of years, at least according to the guy in their recruitment office.

At the same time, I was calling every airline I could think of: Delta, United, Eastern, TWA and American. No one I was able to get hold of wanted to talk to female pilots even though a few of the majors had already start hiring women the year before, in 1973, the year I took my first flight lesson. The two words, "female" and "pilot" just didn't seem to go together. Period. Worse yet, there was currently a severe hiring drought still going on with many of the majors. I was told that so many pilots had been furloughed that it would be a few years, if not longer, before the airlines would be hiring pilots again.

In any case, I was not yet qualified to fly for a major airline; I needed further training that was too expensive in planes I could never have afforded to rent. I needed to fly large airplanes and I needed to find a way to keep flying anything at all while I waited for the furloughs to lift, or the Air Force to come to its senses, or the Navy program to open up. There was no indication that any of those things was likely to happen in the near future.

Although I had my instructor's license, I had no desire to teach when what I wanted to do was fly. I did take on a student or two, but it just wasn't what I wanted. I enjoyed teaching, but it wasn't the same as flying myself. Whatever obstacles were in my way at that time, I wasn't going to stop until I was flying for a commercial airline, preferably United.

I took a job spotting Marlin by air off the coast of California for sports fishermen, but I quit after two days. I felt too sorry for the fish and couldn't handle the guilt.

"Why not become a stewardess," one particularly unimaginative airlines human resources executive told me. "You'll never get into the air force, and the airlines just aren't going to hire girl pilots."

I had nothing against stewardesses, but I was a pilot. "You don't tell a surgeon to become a nurse," I informed him. "Why should I be a stewardess?"

"Because that's what women in aviation do, and you want to be in aviation."

So much in society was transforming in the early seventies, yet while the number of women entering various professions was increasing exponentially year after year, the vast majority of people's attitudes remained frozen in the 1950's.

If I was going to get where I wanted to go, I couldn't waste my time trying to convince someone to give me a chance. Instead, I had to find another way to become so accomplished that no one could turn me down on account of experience or gender. My gender had not been relevant to achieving my goals up to this point, and I saw no reason why it should start now.

Bessie Coleman, the first black female pilot, had to leave the United States in order to obtain her pilot's license. There's almost always a way of getting where you want to go; you sometimes just have to look in places other people don't. I realized that my life had taken on a theme: never take "no" for an answer. Fortunately, as it turned out, this came to me quite naturally, and I'd certainly already had some practice.

There was nothing left to do but make one more call. The Army, it turned out, said it would be happy to have me. That's because they didn't know any better. At the time I called, they had no female pilots at all but were looking for their first one. It wasn't at all what I had in mind; flying for the Army meant primarily flying helicopters, which would add nothing if anything to an airline applicant's resume as far as I could tell. I needed to do something, though, for a few years, to let some time pass and go fly something, somewhere, while waiting out the airline hiring freeze. I figured I could go fly fixed-wing airplanes on the side.

In the winter of 1974, I enlisted in the Army and headed off for two months of boot camp at Fort McClellan in Anniston, Alabama. My term was to be for just three years with an option to re-enlist. I cut a deal with them that I was to go through their entire Air Traffic Control program, which I thought would be a nice education, and then, rather than actually go be a controller, move right into flight school. The Army had no problem with that arrangement.

I had a problem, however, with the fact that the Army had nothing worth flying in terms of building the experience needed to be seriously considered for an airline job, but at the time I didn't have any better solutions. But helicopters sounded like fun, and I could always try for their fixed-wing program later. They didn't fly anything very large, but they did fly the C-12, the designation for the King Air, a nice turbo-prop.

My parents were pretty horrified at the thought of my joining the Army, but they were used to startling announcements by that time. So, off I went.

*How hard can this be?* I thought to myself as I headed off on two-weeks' leave only days after I'd arrived to begin boot camp. The first day, lined up for formation we were offered a choice: stay and "paint toilets in the field" or take a two-week leave. I looked to the girl next to me quizzically. "Why would anyone paint toilets in a field?" I whispered. She just widened her eyes and shook her head.

I decided to find a plane and head home for the holidays. It would be a nice surprise for my parents, and I wouldn't have to learn what toilets in the field were, at least not right away. "Mom," I called her that night, "make sure you're home on the twentieth. I'm sending you something."

I rented a Cherokee 6, a single-engine six-seater, from a Fixed Base Operator at a local airport. To help defray costs, I put up a flyer in my barracks and got a group of girls together who wanted to head west but couldn't afford to fly commercially. In the end, there were six of us: Georgia was headed to Fresno, Winnie to Bakersfield, Lynda to Hawthorne, Kit to Long Beach, and Anne and I would end the air taxi in San Diego.

We took off in the middle of a snowstorm. Needless to say, we didn't get very far before being grounded at an airport in

Monroe, Louisiana—accent on the first syllable. "We all in de South now," Kit drawled in an exaggerated southern accent.

"Monroe Tower," I radioed, "Cherokee 121 Mike Lima at the marker." We had just been handed off by Approach Control.

"Cherokee 121 Mike Lima, cleared to land." There was a hint of confusion in the voice that responded to my call, but I didn't think much about it until the tower radioed again as we taxied in. "Cherokee 121 Mike Lima, you want to come on up and say hello? We don't get many female pilots down 'round here."

I turned to my passengers. "Ladies, we've been invited up to the tower. Shall we?" Dressed in our Class-A uniforms (Army dress uniform with skirt, blouse and blazer) we were a sight. I had insisted that we all travel in our Class-A uniforms because I knew we'd be treated differently than we would have in jeans and jackets. That, combined with the fact that six young women, and not one, walked through the tower doors, inspired an impromptu party. One of the guys went out and got chips, dip, and soft drinks. We sat about for hours talking.

The next morning we took off again but continued to be plagued by bad weather, which forced us to stop at a number of airports along the way in Texas, Oklahoma and New Mexico—more stops than would have been necessary had we just needed to refuel. Finally, we got to Fresno, delivering Georgia safely. Winnie got to Bakersfield in good time, but we arrived at Hawthorne at two in the morning, and got stuck behind locked gates. Not to be deterred at this point, we climbed the fence and spent the night at Lynda's parents' house. The next morning I delivered Kit to Long Beach. Finally, Anne and I arrived in San Diego, and gave my parents the surprise I'd intended. And I was only four days late!

"Meryl," my mom said as I came through the front door, "help me set the table for dinner." She didn't miss a beat.

While at home, the *San Diego Union* did a story about our flight. Apparently Anne had alerted them to our trek unbeknownst to me. The newspaper sent a photographer out to Gillespie Field, where I'd parked the airplane, and they took several pictures, one of which wound up on the front page of a section of the Sunday paper. I was surprised when a few people actually recognized me from the newspaper photo, in which I'd posed on the wing of my airplane in my Army uniform.

Almost as soon as I arrived home it was time to turn around, pick up all the girls—except Anne, who'd decided to find her own way back to buy more time at home—and make the return trip to Fort McClellan. The first part of the way back was smooth, but we ran into a serious snag in Dallas at Love Field. As I did my preflight walkaround I noticed something that would have been disastrous had I not seen it. There was a visible crack in the propeller. Somehow, between New Mexico and Dallas the crack had formed. I was grateful we'd had to land for refueling, as we would have surely lost the propeller in the air.

Immediately I got a mechanic. He took a look and clicked his tongue, then disappeared into a hangar. The girls and I milled about in front of our injured plane. A few minutes later, the mechanic emerged. I bit my nails. "There's an AD note on this particular propeller," he said. "There's a weak spot which has been identified and makes the propeller prone to splitting. It'll take at least ten days to get a propeller. You're lucky it didn't come apart on you in flight." With that, he turned on his heel and headed back to the shop, leaving us staring after him in disbelief.

Everyone groaned and threw up their hands. Winnie asked, "What's an 'AD note'?"

"An FAA Airworthiness Directive," I answered with a sigh. "It means we're grounded—or at least the plane is." I had no idea what to do, but I took a look at the situation and was determined to figure something out. I *had* to figure something out since I was the pilot. I could feel the girls' eyes on me as I paced back and forth. "Okay," I stopped short and turned to my passengers, careful to keep my tone even. "We've all get to get back to Anniston before leave's up. And it's up tomorrow at 0700." *How am I going to manage this?* I asked myself.

As if on cue, Lynda set her hands on her hips and asked "And how, Meryl, are we supposed to do that?"

I smiled. "I'm glad you asked. Don't worry, I'll take care of it." I started pacing around in front of the plane again. Obviously, we weren't going anywhere in this airplane. "Anniston Airport is closest to base. I'll try to get you rides there, and if not, as close as possible. From there you'll have to find a bus or a cab, or ask for a ride to base."

"What about you?" Winnie asked me.

I looked at Winnie. "I'll figure something out. I took you on, and I'll see that you all get back to base on time. Wait here. I'm going to the control tower to get some help."

It wasn't that hard finding rides for five women in uniform. Up in the control tower, I found the Tower Chief and told him our sad story. He was happy to help.

"Don't you worry, Meryl, we'll have your girls in the air in no time." He had a controller put out the word to planes calling for initial taxi clearance. "Tell 'em that some Army ladies need a lift to Alabama." As each plane called up for taxi, the tower explained our situation and, before long, each girl had a lift.

I headed back downstairs and said my good-byes to my friends. "You'll be okay?" Winnie asked, concern in her voice.

"I'll be fine. See you at formation tomorrow morning," I said with a weak grin.

I saw the girls off and then found the mechanic. "May I use your phone to call my FBO?"

"Sure. It's in the office. Close the door when you're done; I'm heading home."

I figured I'd let the Fixed Base Operator know what had happened and, like any car rental agency, they'd arrange to pick the plane up or have it delivered once the plane was fixed. I was wrong.

"What do you *mean* I have to get it home after it's fixed?" I shouted into the phone. "*I* didn't break it!" Great. Not only did I have to find my way back to base, I'd have to find my way back *again* to Love Field to fetch the plane. I sighed, and slumped down in the chair. Well, first things first. Now that my friends were all accounted for, it was my turn to get back to base. But with nightfall setting in, the number of planes coming in to Love Field was thinning out. I closed the door to the mechanic's office and made my way back up to the tower.

A few guys were sitting about relaxing. Air traffic hadn't just thinned out—it had all but stopped. "Well, this is not look-ing promising," I said to no one in particular. "I'm AWOL if I don't make it to roll call in the morning."

The Tower Chief who'd been so accommodating put a com-forting arm around me. "Why don't you go see Jim? He might know someone heading out. Try Hangar Three, way in the back there."

I left the tower once again and headed down to the hangars. Most were dark, but one had a light in the back and I could hear the sound of intermittent voices. The cadence was easy and unhurried, and it felt inviting. "Hello?" I called as I made my way toward the voices. As I approached, I could hear the sound of clicking and a crack, and then laughter.

At the back of the hangar was a large office—more like a men's lodge than an office, well appointed with couches and stuffed animal heads on the wall. A bare bulb hung from a low ceiling, illuminating a full-sized pool table. Three men stood about shooting pool. "Hello?" I said again. "I'm looking for Jim."

They looked up in surprise. "Yeah," a heavyset man with gray hair said in that 'who's asking?' tone of voice. "That's me."

I stepped forward and held out my hand. "The guys in the tower told me I might find you here. My name's Meryl Getline."

He shook my hand. "Meryl."

I looked to the other two men and smiled.

Jim pointed at another man, large like Jim, only taller. "This here's Doug."

Doug held out his hand. "Miss Getline."

"And this," he gestured to the third man, a tall, strapping man wearing a cowboy hat low on his brow, "is Roger."

Roger looked up and I gasped audibly. "The Marlboro Man!" (Yes, the real one from all the ads.)

He smiled and tipped his hat. "Ma'am."

The Marlboro Man and Doug turned back to their game, and Jim began chalking his cue. "So," Jim said blowing the dust off the cue tip, "what do you need?" Doug racked the table again and Roger broke it. Jim walked around to the other side of the table to size up his shot.

"I'm trying to get back to Alabama. I've got a seven AM report time tomorrow in Alabama, at Fort McClellan, but my plane is grounded. I'm a little short on time."

Doug looked up. "Grounded?"

"Yeah. A crack in the propeller. I was with friends, but I found them rides."

"Who all's piloting?" Doug asked.

"Me. I'm the pilot."

Jim stopped in the middle of his shot. "You don't say. You're a little young, aren't you?"

"No," I said matter-of-factly.

"I'll give you a lift," Jim said with the beginning of a smile.

My face lit up. I'd make it back in time after all! "I'd really appreciate it."

"But not for free." He broke into a full smile.

My face fell. "But I don't have any money. I spent it all just trying to get home and back."

"Tell you what. We'll play a game of pool and bet the price of the gas."

"Pool? I can't play pool. I don't know how."

Jim sighed. "Well now, that's too bad."

Roger had leaned back against the table, crossing his ankles. He looked just like he did in the cigarette ads. Now he just needed to light up a Marlboro to complete the picture, but he was smoking another brand.

"Hey, that's not a Marlboro. How come?"

He looked at me out of the corner of his eye. "I never could stand 'em."

Doug chimed in. "How 'bout poker? Play you a game of poker for the ride."

I thought for a second. What did I have to lose except money I didn't have? Besides, my three older brothers had taught me a couple of things. One of them was basketball. Another was poker. Thank God. "Sure, okay."

We pulled chairs up to a folding table and Jim found some chips and cards. "Best two out of three," Jim suggested.

I won. And handily, I might add.

"Three out of five," he challenged.

"I really need to get back," I protested.

A slow rumble started with Jim, and erupted into full-blown, tear-stained laughter. Doug and Roger weren't far behind.

"What?" I demanded. "What's so funny?"

Finally, Jim managed to speak. "Oh, Meryl, you're a good sport." He wiped his eyes.

I was annoyed. "Well, I'm glad I amuse you."

"Aw, come on now," he continued. "We were always going to give you a ride. I just wanted to see if you could play."

Despite myself, I started to laugh, too. "Well I sure kicked your butt, didn't I?"

"Yes, Ma'am, you did," Jim laughed, and gathered up the cards. "So, boys, shall we escort this lovely lady home?"

We all piled into a Golden Eagle, a beautiful light twin, otherwise known as a Cessna-421, and took off. It turned out that Doug was an FAA inspector and Jim ran a commercial and corporate transport company called Western Jet. The Marlboro Man was apparently between ads. The entire flight to Alabama we talked aviation. By the time we reached Anniston at three in the morning, we'd exchanged numbers and Jim promised to call if he had any openings for copilots. *I do have weekends free*, I thought, and would worry about how to get to Dallas later.

I got out and thanked my new friends. As I began to close the door, Jim said, "Meryl, you sure got some moxie."

I grinned. "And you've got some sense of humor."

"Welcome to aviation!"

I made it back to base before leave ended. It would turn out to be the first of many occasions in my military tenure when I made it back just in the nick of time.

Looking back, I thought, my first adventure in the military wasn't all that bad. After all, I'd been given leave as soon as I enlisted, then spent that leave almost entirely in the air. That trip would set the stage for the remainder of my time in the Army.

Recently I came across a letter my father sent to me while I was at Fort McClellan. "Dear Peripatetic Pussycat," he wrote, "I am convinced that the Army exists for your personal convenience." My father has always been an astute man.

## CHAPTER 14

## Fatigues and Green Tennies

I had no illusions about Army life. My reasons for being there did not involve a long-term career in the military. Having said that, however, I did put forth an effort. I just wasn't very good at it. In fact, I was utterly inept as a soldier. Nevertheless, I was very good at creating the illusion of competence in basic soldiering.

Putting my entrepreneurial instincts to work, I learned that, for a minor fee I could get others to do what I simply could not stand the thought of doing, and couldn't do as well as others, such as shine my shoes, keep lint off my uniform, make a bed you could bounce a quarter off of in military fashion, and organize my locker. And while I wouldn't call my performance as a soldier stellar, I did manage to accomplish some tasks. Our barracks had wall-to-wall carpeting, so I didn't have to scrub floors. Vacuuming was something I could do. I didn't particularly mind it and, as an added attraction, it was difficult to screw up.

As I mentioned, the fee was small: peanut M&Ms purchased at the PX, but those M&Ms were as good as gold. My fellow soldiers were practically addicted to them, along with other treasures from the PX, mainly because there was this silly rule that we weren't allowed to buy anything from there. I decided that, since the rule didn't say anything about eating M&Ms should they happen to appear, nor that we couldn't hang out near the PX, nor anything about someone authorized to purchase from the PX, I had some wiggle room.

Like a kid who gets an adult to buy him a pack of cigarettes, I got others to buy me the peanut M&Ms, which I then distributed to my various valets, who were thrilled to receive them. For a minor additional fee I also started importing various other luxury items from the forbidden PX: cosmetics, shampoos, soaps, candy, and the like.

This arrangement did not always succeed. I had to dock my housekeeper several M&Ms on one occasion for mismanaging my locker. I had a pair of flannel pajamas with a monkey on the front. On one inspection the pajamas were pressed and hung in my locker, but apparently not correctly, according to Army standards. I actually hadn't known that the Army had standards for monkeys. My demerit read, "monkey facing wrong way in wall locker." It was difficult to stifle my laughter as my Commanding Officer explained to me the cause for the demerit while all the girls were openly snickering. I wrote to my mother about it. She had given me those pajamas, and to this day laughs helplessly if I mention the incident to her.

Sometimes my failures were not my fault. The Army didn't have my size in combat boots when I first arrived, so while they were ordering them I had to wear tennis shoes. Jumping over a swamp one day while taking a shortcut back from the PX laden with M&Ms, I misjudged the distance and fell in. I stumbled out with vomit-green tennis shoes. I tried like crazy to get them white again, but to no avail. So, while everyone stood outside in formation for inspection, I was the one, in the midst of a small sea of spit-shined black boots reflecting in the sunlight, wearing drab green tennies. It was too much to hope for that my C.O. would overlook them, and he didn't.

Stopping in front of me, he first looked down at my shoes, then at me, straight in the eyes. "What happened to your shoes, soldier?"

"I fell into a swamp, Sir."

He took a step back and looked down. "Looks like someone threw up on them."

"Yes, Sir," I responded helplessly.

He moved on.

I got used to the other girls fighting desperately to keep from laughing whenever we had formation. There were often guests—other officers—doing the inspections, and invariably I got comments about my shoes. My specially ordered combat boots would not catch up with me until a few weeks after I arrived at my next training base, Fort Rucker.

The Army forces people like me to make full use of their resourcefulness. As everyone knows, boot camp is synonymous with getting yelled at by drill sergeants while running endless miles in horrible conditions. My experience was no different. What I did manage to do, however, was locate the best hiding spots so that, like the cheating marathon runner, I could break off from formation and hide out until the troops passed by on their way back to camp. During one physical fitness test, my friend Kathy and I broke off from the group—it wasn't difficult, considering we were lagging miserably behind anyway—and hid behind a tree until the group came back and we could fall in behind them.

Of course, such escapades—a euphemism my drill sergeant would not likely use—did not endear me to Army regulars. My drill sergeant, in particular, was less than thrilled with me. Drill Sergeant Roberts was, I thought, just horrible: demanding, loud, irritating—everything a drill sergeant was supposed to be. It didn't bother me much that she didn't like me. Drill Sergeant

Roberts, a.k.a., Bitch from Hell, had early on decided—and rightly so, I must say—that I was not soldier material.

She never caught me running my PX scheme, but she'd seen the flyer I'd put up advertising for passengers, and later saw the *San Diego Union* article Anne had posted on the barrack's bulletin board. I was, in her mind, a rabble-rouser and not nearly deferential enough. Although I would take issue with the former characterization, I do admit to a deficiency with appropriate salutations. More than once I forgot to salute a superior officer or address my C. O. properly.

Hopeless as I was in most areas of soldiering, I was a naturally good shot when it came to qualifying on the M-16 rifle as part of the boot camp requirement. When others asked my secret, I would reply nonchalantly, "Nothing to it. I just pretend Drill Sergeant Roberts is the target." It was true, and I rarely missed my shot.

Needless to say, Drill Sergeant Roberts always kept a special eye out for me, and in the fishbowl that is boot camp, further scrutiny made the experience particularly oppressive. I didn't relish asking permission, then, when Love Field called to tell me the Cherokee was ready for pick-up. But I didn't have much choice, either, and she reluctantly gave me permission to fetch the plane.

Though I was excited to fly again, I was initially annoyed at having to pick up a plane I hadn't broken to begin with. But that trip to Love Field, combined with my earlier impromptu hitchhiking with Jim—not to mention finding rides for all "my girls"—made me realize how surprisingly easy it was to hitch rides by plane all over the country. I started out by car, hitching a ride to Anniston airport. I got a flight instructor to include a stop at Birmingham Airport in a flight lesson he was giving. From there I hitched a ride on a corporate plane straight to

Dallas. I made such good time getting there that I was able to stop by and say "hi" to Jim and company in Hangar Three.

The ride back to Anniston was smooth, taking only about four hours. Someone from the FBO gave me a ride back to base. Hitching rides on civilian and military airplanes, supplemented by a minor amount of hitchhiking by ground, was proving to be a great way to travel, and I would later take full advantage of it.

After I returned from Dallas I didn't get to do much weekend traveling. I did, however, get one or two day trips in. We'd be granted leave for the day, for example, but had to report in for curfew the same night.

On one such day of leave, the company from whom I had rented the Cherokee Six for the flight to California called me at my barracks and asked if I wouldn't mind giving a ride to a man headed to Birmingham. He would pay the cost, of course. The idea of having passengers was always appealing to me. I liked having people to take safely from one place to another. So I agreed.

He was a big man, an old man, who had trouble getting into the small two-seater airplane. When finally secured, we headed off for Birmingham under cloudy skies. It was a short flight, and with the weather worsening, I didn't have time to make small talk along the way.

Paying attention to the flight, I didn't notice my passenger nodding off. Suddenly, there was a head in my lap. "Excuse me!" I started to exclaim, but as I was saying it, I realized he was passed out—or worse.

Trying to lift his head with one hand, and hold the yoke to steer with the other, I couldn't feel any breath or make out a pulse.

"Okay, okay." I scrambled to rearrange him, where I could better assess his condition. I pushed my seat back and managed to turn him over so he was face-up, his head propped against the window on my side of the cockpit. He wasn't breathing that I could tell, but I was finally able to find a pulse, and would have breathed a sigh of relief but there wasn't time. I had to begin mouth-to-mouth resuscitation. I lifted my knees and braced them to support his torso, and then reached for the airplane's microphone, which had fallen to the floor when he fell on me.

Moments earlier, I had reached my cruising altitude and was already in contact with Houston Center, which had control over the airspace over Alabama. I radioed, "Houston, Cessna-4122 Delta. I have a passenger that's passed out, a possible heart attack. I need to turn around and proceed directly back to Anniston for landing. I'm declaring an emergency and will need paramedics to meet us."

Without waiting for a response, I leaned over and began mouth-to-mouth. This would have been a good time to have an autopilot, but this was just a little Cessna-150 and there wasn't one, so I managed the best I could, making periodic corrections to my course and altitude.

*Please don't remember this when you wake up,* I prayed. Nothing. I tried again. Nothing. And again. A breath!

He suddenly gasped and moaned a little, and then I made a most unpleasant discovery regarding what can happen when one wakes up in this manner: he threw up. Big-time. All over my Class-A uniform.

It was all I could do not to vomit myself, so awful was the smell when it hit my nose. I managed to check that my passenger was still breathing, and then opened the small window next to me, pressing my face up against it to catch glorious, clean lungs-full of frigid air.

Though the air was terribly cold, and the rain was driving right into my face, at least I could breathe. I'd stick my nose out, grab some air, and then pull back in to check my passenger. When it looked like he was doing okay breathing on his own, I kept the side of my face pressed against the ice-cold window.

It wasn't long before I began shivering, and I knew my passenger must be cold, too. There was no way I was going to shut that window, but I was concerned that my passed-out passenger could become hypothermic even with the airplane's heater going full-blast. I glanced at his face and was very alarmed to see how utterly pale—almost blue—he was. With some difficulty, I shimmied out of my jacket and wrapped it around his shoulders. Next, I propped him up and, still clutching the yoke, struggled out of my skirt and my blouse, and wrapped those around him, too, vomit and all. I had no other way to try and keep him from freezing to death. Finally, sitting in my underwear and heels, I stuck my nose out the window again.

"Anniston tower, this is Cessna-4122 Delta."

"Cessna-4122 Delta, we have paramedics standing by for you. Cleared to land."

We were met by a swarm of emergency vehicles, including fire truck, ambulance, and police. I'll never forget the look on the paramedic's face as he opened the door and an almost-naked woman came out.

I was given a blanket and ushered into the ambulance with my passenger, and we were whisked away to the hospital, where I waited to be checked out in the Emergency Room while my passenger was whisked behind closed doors.

"You should really stay overnight for observation," the ER doctor said to me.

I knew I was cold, but in the chaos hadn't realized that I, too, was at risk for hypothermia. "I can't," I protested. "I need my uniform back. I've got curfew! Anyway, I'm fine."

He relented, and I was able to get cleaned up and was given a hospital smock to wear while I waited to get my uniform back.

After a few hours the ER doctor told me that the man would be okay, that indeed, he'd had a heart attack. "If you hadn't acted…" his voice trailed off, full of meaning.

I went to the nurse's station to see about the status of my uniform.

A heavyset woman with no-nonsense eyes sat before me, her eyebrows arched and lips pursed. "So, you want your uniform back, the one with vomit all over it?"

I nodded.

"The one you took off to put on the man who threw up on you in the first place?" she continued.

"Well, yes," I stumbled, "but you make it sound, uh, weird. I mean, I didn't put it *on* him…" In the midst of the expression on her face, I had nothing else to say.

"Honey," she clucked her tongue, waving a finger at me, "you don't want that thing back."

"I know, you're right. Normally, I'd say throw it out. But it's my military uniform. What would I tell them?"

She shook her head in that world-weary sort of way, and said, "Hang on. I'll go see if I can't find it," and she shuffled through a door behind her.

I had to have my uniform. I couldn't go back to base without it. If nothing else, Drill Sergeant Roberts was always checking that my uniform was either on my person or in my locker looking pristine. I didn't relish her finding out about my most recent extra-curricular activities. The less she knew about what I did with my time off base the better.

The woman re-emerged, hands up to show she didn't have it. "It's gotta be 'round here somewhere," she offered. "I'm sure it went with the man up to his room. He's admitted by now, so maybe the nurses got it up with him."

"No one in the ER remembers the uniform?" I asked in disbelief.

"Sweetheart, your suit is not the worst thing we've ever seen."

I sighed, and she checked his room number for me. Then I headed upstairs. I looked in on my passenger, who was resting comfortably, and then proceeded to the nurse's station on his floor. No luck. Not in his room, not in storage on his floor.

"You could try the laundry," one nurse offered. "Stuff like that often goes for cleaning."

It was now late Sunday night, and I had to get back to base. I trudged down to the hospital's laundry center, muttering in resignation, "It's got to be *dry* cleaned."

To my relief, it was dry cleaned, hanging amongst other clothes, with my passenger's room number pinned to the sleeve. After some negotiating and profuse thanks I was able to retrieve it and escape back to base. A nurse just going off-duty offered me a ride back to base, which I gladly accepted.

Normally, from the front gate of the base, I'd talk an MP (Military Police) into giving me a ride to my barracks. They'd long ago stopped asking questions about where I was going all the time. That night the guy giving me the ride said, "Wait 'till you see what you missed!" But he wouldn't say any more than that.

As we drove up to my barracks, a group of women was being led away by some other MP's. Among them was my Drill Sergeant Roberts! Other soldiers, both male and female, stood about watching the scene.

"What's going on?" I asked.

One turned to me and replied, "Arrested. About forty of them."

I was dumbfounded. "Why in the world…?"

"Inappropriate behavior," he said knowingly.

"Inappropriate behavior," I said, wrapping my brain around the meaning.

"Yup. I guess it's not a myth what they say about women in the military."

I clutched my newly dry-cleaned jacket, pulling it tight around my neck. "*I'm* a woman in the military."

"Yeah, well…"

I hadn't suspected it, but then again, had no reason to suspect. But I must say, Drill Sergeant Roberts was a bit of a surprise. Still, I was glad to see her go. Under the circumstances, I didn't think she'd be back, and I was right. Shaking my head, I waited until the activity subsided, and then went to my barracks, now significantly less populated. Up until then I'd thought *I* was the one having a rough day.

My new drill sergeant was a large black man. He was no less forbidding than Roberts, but at least he didn't have a particular dislike for me. To be fair, he was all business, singling nobody out for either favoritism or extra criticism.

When I went back a few days later on a weekend leave to check on my passenger, who was recovering nicely, I had to be doubly careful under the watchful eyes of Drill Sergeant Maxwell. I felt I'd been given a new chance to make a good impression, or at least avoid a negative one, and I didn't want to blow it. I made certain that the rest of my sojourn at boot camp remained relatively uneventful—no easy task for me, by the way.

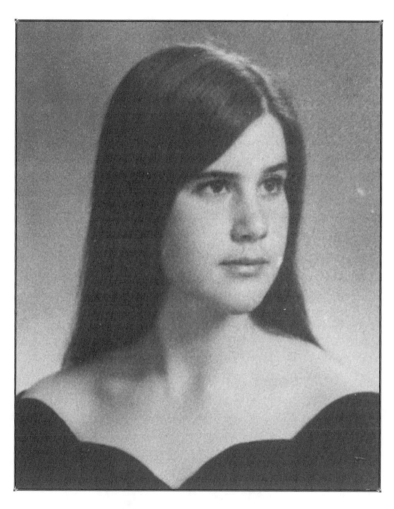

My 10th grade yearbook picture, taken at age 15.

Toba, My Iranian friend, helped me hide from the beach police when we went swimming and windsurfing at the Caspian Sea. Women were not allowed to wear bathing suits in public.

Mr. Ed Leon, everybody's favorite teacher. He was instrumental in supporting my solo trip to Europe just out of the tenth grade, helping me find a school and a good deal on airfare. He shared my opinion that "total immersion" in learning a foreign language was the only way to go.

SPRECHEN SIE DEUTSCH?
Even the French were nice.

GERMAN IS GERMANE

## She speaks like a native

Printed by local San Diego newspaper, "The Peninsula News"
after my return from Austria. I was 16 year old.

Beautiful Innsbruck, Austria.
The Jordans' house, where I spent the summer, is barely out
of the frame to the left in the foothills of the Alps.

I took this picture near where I took my spill over the cliff in front of
the Jordans' house. You can see how steep these mountains are,
in the foothills of the Austrian Alps.

---

I took this picture of a Bedouin and his camel in the Israeli desert
during my 1969 winter trip. I was in the 11th grade and 16 years old.

Miss Meryl Getline, 21, sits at the controls of the plane she rented to come home here for the holidays from Alabama, where she is in Army boot camp. She started the trip in a snowstorm and took 21 hours flight time.

—Staff photo by Tony Doubek

# One Poster, One New Career

The San Diego Union ran this photo and article in 1974 when I was home on leave from Army. I had arrived for Basic Training just in time for Christmas vacation. I rented a single-engine airplane and six of us Army ladies flew to the west coast for Christmas. I'm 21 years old here.

It was hard to leave family pets when I went away on trips. This is Meredith.

# Around the world in 25 days

I couldn't believe it when the Army granted me additional time off
to go take a trip around the world! This was an article published by
the newspaper at Ft. Rucker, Alabama, where I was in
Air Traffic Control school. I'm 22 years old here.

---

THE DAILY LEDGER, Monday, May 19, 1975 Pa

# WAC hopes to be airline captain

convinced her. It lasted all of
20 minutes - and she became
airsick.

The length of her flights has
increased considerably. (She
said she has crossed the
Atlantic 14 times - 16 times
following her current trip.)
And Meryl has a talent for
getting those flights - not
especially across the Atlantic,
though.

She is a hitchhiker ex-
traordinary. "I discovered a
few months ago that if you
want to go somewhere by air,
you just have to get to an
airport, find a pilot who will
give you a ride, and take off."

On her weekend jaunts,
many of which begin in
Montgomery, Ala., the
destination is not really important , she said.    What
matters is that she is in the air
and logging flight time.

A Getline weekend rec..
went like this:     Satu..
morning to Denver, Colo..
an Air Force jet;  Su..
morning she caught a ri..
Trenton, N. J. (one of..
fellow passengers was a th..
star general), and from t..
Orlando, Fla., to Atla..
Ga.

The weekend was not a..
success, Meryl said, bec..
she had to "travel by grou..
to get back to Ft. Rucke..
time for classes Mon..
morning.

So now Pvt. Getline i..
the really big trip. ..
question, though, is whe..
she will stay with ..
scheduled airline flights ..
be just a passenger (prob..
a sick one) or whether she..
get out and hitch a ride f..
London to Paris.

A local Alabama newspaper.
Here the focus is on my intent to become an airline captain.

Here I am posing for another newspaper article, sitting on the wing of the Cherokee I rented in Alabama and flew, with five of my Army boot camp buddies, to the West Coast for my first Army Christmas leave.

**ON THE JOB**

(Times Photos by Mike Somoilli)

Meryl Gettine flies her Swearingen "Metroliner" on a schedule that starts and ends at her company's main operating base in Visalia. She is one of 16 pilots who fly for the commuter line that moved into the central state as the larger airlines pulled out.

# She is, indeed, an airline captain

The title states I was an airline captain, which was true, but it's certainly not what I had in mind. What I had in mind was becoming a captain for United Airlines which eventually, of course, I did.

I just never knew whom I'd run into on my "Soldier of Fortune" weekends, where I pretty much went wherever the wind blew me, so to speak. Here I am flying around with none other than Alabama Governor George Wallace. His wife, Cornelia took the picture.

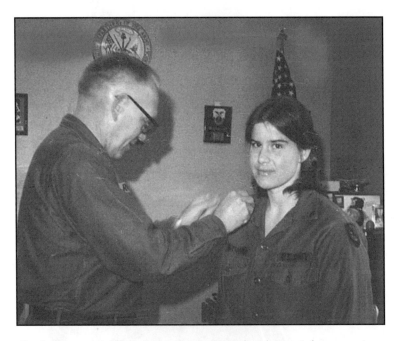

Getting promoted from Private 1 to Specialist 4—a triple promotion.
Not too bad for someone as inept as I was at being a soldier.

This careless camel in Turkey caused some interesting moments during an inspection back at Ft. Rucker.

YOU ARE HERE.

Buzzing Smokey Joe's. I told my brother Ned, the owner, about what time to expect us. There he is in front with his clientele. This same picture still hangs on the wall today at Smokey Joe's Café in Berkeley, California.

I decided to skip the Army's helicopter program as it was too restrictive with respect to flying fixed-wing aircraft, but I couldn't resist getting a civilian helicopter rating anyway while I was still in the Army. I got plenty of flight time in Army helicopters before and after I got my civilian rating, courtesy of guys who let me fly while they were out getting their required flight hours in each month. I'd tag along and take over for awhile.

# Meryl Gets High
# On Her Ambition

Female helicopter
pilots were at least as
unusual as female
fixed-wing pilots. The
Oakland Tribune did
this story during my
first civilian flight
lesson (I'd already had
plenty of unauthorized
training in helicopters
from both the Army
and the Navy by then).
Astro-Copters of
Oakland had never
had a female helicopter
student before.
That's Barry Lloyd,
my instructor, shown
with me.

Hoppy and me in front of Channing Clark's 1936 Fleetwings Seabird, the only airworthy one of its type of six that were built. Hoppy was a tremendous help in getting me the multi-engine time I needed to get an airline job.

---

Channing Clark on his Fleetwings Seabird, also known as the "SST," which stood for Stainless Steel Tub. Chan referred to himself as an "Aerial Yachtsman." Chan would put up financing for the Iranian twin-engine aircraft I tried to help purchase.

Dick Maple, Chief Pilot for Inland Empire Airlines and former Iran
Air pilot. He found three Navajo Chieftains—the type of plane
Inland Empire was flying at the time—for sale at a great price in Iran.
Unbeknownst to him, I was planning to come along.

This is one of the Chieftains for sale, being operated by the Iranian
regional airline Pars Air (short for "Persian Air Service).

One of the Fokker F-28's that the Dutch wanted me to help confiscate and return to Holland. While I was in the neighborhood, I flew copilot around Iran with Luis flying as captain for Pars Air.

---

Some of my fellow pilots at Inland Empire Airlines.
Behind is one of the company's Metroliners.
Left to right: Brad Silverman (now a United Airlines captain),
Mike Beaver, me, Dave Pugh, Russ Hildebrand and Bob Carlton.

In my Inland Empire Uniform just after Inland Empire
moved its base to Fresno, California.

# SHE FLIES . . .
# INLAND SKIES

Vivacious twenty-six year old Inland Empire Airlines Captain, Meryl Getline, has over six years of pilot experience and has logged more than 4,500 hours of flying time. She flies one of Inland's 19-seat prop jet Metroliner aircraft manufactured by Swearingen, a Division of Fairchild Industries) which cruises at 300 MPH. Metroliners are built in San Antonio, Texas, where she took her simulator training for that aircraft.

Born in Dayton, Ohio, the youngest of four children, she and her family moved to San Diego where she attended San Diego State University, majoring in linguistics. She converses fluently in French and German and is extremely accomplished on the piano and violin. While attending college she also took flying instructions, her first love. "Since early childhood," Meryl related. "I knew that some day I would be a commercial pilot."

Leaving school, she enlisted in the United States Army for a three-year tour of duty and was stationed at Fort Ord, California, as an Air Traffic Controller.

After completing her tour in the military she embarked on her career in commercial aviation. Inland's Chief Pilot, Dale Tregoning (L), said Captain Getline has an excellent relationship with her co-workers and is a valuable asset to Inland's staff of highly trained pilots.

Captain Meryl Getline

## INLAND EXPANDS SERVICE

Inland Empire Airlines is finalizing a major expansion of service for the Fresno-area traveling public, it was announced recently.

Joseph Healey, president of IEA, and Douglas Crowther, general manager, stated that starting July 1, Inland Empire will offer nine daily non-stop round trip flights from Fresno to San Francisco and seven from Fresno to Los Angeles. Currently, IEA offers five flights daily from Fresno to San Francisco and Los Angeles.

and May. We feel extremely confident that our new July 1 schedule of seven flights to Los Angeles and nine to San Francisco will also elicit a very positive public response." Healey added.

"Adding San Jose, Oakland and Ontario to the IEA system is the result of some careful analysis of destination cities in California that would provide good, long term, two-way traffic for our business traveler as well as the passenger connecting with other airlines or

---

Lady pilots for airlines—even small commuters like Inland Empire—
were still unusual at that time. I didn't personally know a single one
other than myself; hence the large number of newspaper articles.
Here I am in the cockpit of one of Inland's Metroliners.
That's Dale Tregoning, Inland Empire's Chief Pilot with me
in the other picture. Dale went with me to get his flight
engineer's rating at United Airlines' Training Center in Denver
in 1980 about a month after this article was published.

By the United DC-10 the day of my checkride.
Left to right: Tom Speer, at that time a technical writer for United,
who later became a pilot and trainer in the DC-10 fleet at United,
Tommy Thompson, the FAA inspector who gave Dale and me
our check rides, me, Jerry Warnke, my DC-10 flight instructor,
and Mike Grott, a flight manager with United.

## Jumbo jet wings for pilot, 27

By GENE KUHN
Bee staff writer

At 27, Meryl Getline may the youngest pilot to qualify for a DC-10 captain's rating in a world in which the average age is 54.

To top it off, she also holds a flight engineer's rating in the same jet.

Getline regularly flies considerably smaller aircraft — 19-passenger Metroliners for Inland Empire Airlines.

"Flying in and out of Los Angeles and San Francisco, we're surrounded by jumbo jets," she said. "I just love those big jets. They really turn me on."

So on her 27th birthday on June 26, she decided to do something about it, to give herself an extravagant present "from me to me."

Inland Empire Airlines pilot Meryl Getline in the seat of a Metroliner.

Fresno Bee

Just back from getting my DC-10 Flight Engineer
and DC-10 Type Rating (Captain's Rating).

Flying the San Franciso 49'ers on a Superbowl Charter.
One of United's flight managers took it upon himself to have
United's paint scheme modified! United kept the paint job for years.

My very first flight for Wien Air Alaska, on my 28th birthday, was this photo shoot around Mt. McKinley. Several shots were utilized in magazine and newspaper advertising for Wien. I'm in the B-727, the jet closest to the mountain. A Learjet flew alongside taking the pictures.

---

As a flight engineer for Wien Air Alaska. I'd make it to the copilot's position, but not the captain's seat before they went out of business.

Captain at LAST on a United Airlines B-727.

An all female crew on the B-727.
Flight Attendants Files, Simpkins and Poulton,
Second Officer Staples, First Officer Kerly and me,
Captain Getline, on September 8, 1994.

Picture taken when I was flying into Hartford,
Connecticut was taken by another United Airlines pilot.

Captain Al Carmickle on approach to Hong Kong in one of United's
gorgeous B-747-400's, taken by a first officer on a layover in Hong Kong.
It's the airplane I hope to fly before I retire.

DC-10 Training Check Captain Al Carmickle was my check pilot
for my upgrade from flight engineer to copilot.
He later became my Significant Other.

My parents celebrated their 60th wedding anniversary on May 16th, 2002. Ned's wife, Irene Imfeld, a graphic designer, put together this small collage for the occasion. The top picture was taken in 1942 just before their wedding, the bottom right just before their 60th wedding anniversary. On the left is a picture of the whole family, taken ten years prior at their 50th anniversary celebration. Left to right: My oldest brother Ned (A.K.A. Smokey Joe), me, my mother Bette, my Dad Gordon, my youngest brother Scott and my middle brother Lorin.

In the cockpit on a United Airbus,
taken by one of my first officers in 2003.

## CHAPTER 15

# Skipping Through School

The best aircraft training in the world is in the United States military. The fact that I had been denied this training with the Air Force (women were still not accepted for flight training in 1974) and the Navy (women were being accepted but there was a waiting list up to two years) was devastating, but it only strengthened my resolve to become so qualified with hours and ratings that no airline could justify not hiring me. I was determined to get flight time whenever, wherever, and however the opportunity presented itself.

I managed to get through boot camp without being kicked out of the Army and had fairly high hopes for my stint at Fort Rucker in southern Alabama. It was time to enter the air traffic control program. After that, I planned to complete the helicopter program so I could then attempt to enter the fixed-wing program. I would have much preferred to skip the helicopter part and go right into fixed-wing training, but the Army flew very few fixed-wing aircraft and nobody got into that program without having first gone through their basic flight school, which was strictly for helicopters.

I'd been flying fixed-wing on my own, of course, for long enough that I expected the fixed-wing part of flight school to be easy. I had no expectations regarding helicopter training, however, other than it sounded very different from fixed-wing flying—and like a lot of fun. I was especially interested in learning NOE, or Nap of the Earth, which is extremely low-level helicopter flying. How exciting to fly level with the tree-tops, or even lower! Nevertheless, I was a bit unenthusiastic about the helicopter program overall only because I did not see it helping me get on with the airlines later. In fact there was a joke that the airlines would actually consider helicopter time to be a negative factor, so different are they from fixed-wing air-craft. I was never really certain whether it was actually a joke.

The very first night at Fort Rucker I found the helicopter base and went along on a training mission. I couldn't under-stand why none of the other girls from my barracks wanted to come along. I wouldn't have missed those nights for anything, and went along several nights per week when I didn't have to study or catch up on sleep.

Although I don't think my reputation preceded me, I found I was no higher on my First Sergeant's list of favorite people than I'd been on either one of my Drill Sergeants' back at Basic Training. But while I had not been able to redeem myself as a soldier in boot camp, I won Outstanding Soldier of the Month at Fort Rucker right off the bat when my Commanding Officer, a pilot himself, learned I was a rated pilot, too. In fact, he would often invite me along on his own training flights, and I accept-ed whenever possible.

When I entered the Controller program at Fort Rucker, my class was informed that the curriculum had just been severely condensed into a much shorter, but much more demanding, course. While the rest of the class groaned aloud, I was silently saying, "Thank God," since I knew I already had at least some of the knowledge from being a pilot. What had once taken sev-eral weeks to complete would now take a mere ten days. It was self-paced study done right in the classroom.

As it turned out, I grossly underestimated the overlap of education between being a pilot and being a controller. On the first day, after just an hour and a half, I closed my book and raised my hand. The instructor, a Lieutenant, said, "Please don't tell me you need a rest break already. We just got here." The class snickered.

"No, Sir," I said.

"Well, what is it then?" he asked, sounding mildly annoyed.

"I'm ready to take the test now, Sir."

"C'mon. Nobody reads that fast."

"No, Sir. I don't need to read it. I already know it."

"What on earth are you talking about, Private?"

"I'm a pilot, Sir. It's all the same material." I half expected that the instructor would already know I was a pilot because of my award, but he didn't know or care about the Outstanding Soldier of the Month.

"What, you mean you've taken a couple of lessons?"

"No, Sir. I have my ratings—all of them."

"What does 'all of them' mean, exactly?"

"Well, almost all of them. I'm not old enough for my Airline Transport Rating yet, and anyway, I'm a few hundred hours short, but," I began ticking off my list of ratings, "I have my Private, Instrument, Commercial, Multi-Engine, Ground Instructor, Certified Flight Instructor and Certified Flight Instructor, Instrument."

He stared at me for a second, then said in a strained voice, "Come with me."

We went next door to a smaller classroom where he handed me the test booklet along with a No. 2 pencil, and told me the test had a limit of three hours. I was done before lunch; the entire test had taken me less than forty-five minutes to complete. The instructor graded the paper as I watched. I'd missed three questions and was mortified. He was astonished.

"Private Getline, you only missed three questions," he said, mystified.

"I know, I'm sorry. There's no excuse, I—"

He held up his hand. "Getline, he said, "you just got the highest score ever achieved on this exam. What do you have to say?"

"Sir, I should have gotten 100% and I'm really irritated." Then I smiled and he laughed.

"Why do you even know what a transmissometer is?" A transmissometer measures horizontal visibility down the runway in low-visibility conditions.

"It's just one of the things an instrument pilot has to know about. Really, Sir, you're giving me too much credit. This is all basic pilot stuff." I pointed to the exam. "I shouldn't have missed any."

Before the day was over, I was called into my Commanding Officer's quarters and informed that I had just received three promotions. I skipped over Private 2, Private 3 (Private First Class), and was suddenly a Specialist 4. Specialist in what, I wasn't quite sure. I had my own opinion of what I was a Specialist of, but it wasn't polite to say. In any case, the Army was pretty loose about its titles.

Despite my success on the exam and a bunch of promotions, I still had things to learn. Passing the written was one thing, but I still needed the hands-on part of the course. I needed radar training, which did not come to me especially easily. I was much better at separating aircraft visually, like they do in control towers.

A week or so after arriving at Fort Rucker I got a call. One of the girls in my barracks told me someone named "Gator" was on the phone. "Getline, you got a Gator on the phone!" she shouted.

*Gator?* I didn't know any Gator. I picked up the receiver. "Hello?"

"Meryl," the voice on the other end boomed. "Jim Geders here."

"Oh, *Jim*, hi!" I'd seen his last name on the business card he'd given me, but I'd never once heard it pronounced aloud.

"How's the Army treating you?"

"Fine. Don't ask me how I'm treating them, though. I think they're still trying to find a way to get rid of me. I can't believe they even graduated me out of Basic. How'd you track me down?"

"Believe me, they remember you at Fort McClellan," he laughed. "Anyway, I have some news for you."

"What?" I asked. "Do you have some flying for me?"

"As a matter of fact, any time you can make it down here you can copilot on one of my planes. But that's not why I called. I called to let you know that I put your name in the hat for an award given by the Pilots Association of Dallas, and you won!"

"I can't believe it! Why would anybody award me anything?" I was astonished.

"I told them about how you got all those ratings in such a short amount of time, how you slept at the airport so you'd get more flight hours, how you got stranded here and found rides back to base for all your friends, and they were impressed."

"Wow, thanks, Jim. That's so nice! Is there a dinner or something, or do you just mail a certificate?"

"Oh, it's a bit more than dinner," he said dryly. Jim, it turns out, was a master of understatement. "But you'll just have to wait to find out. Listen, I have to go, but you'll hear something official in a few days. Great to hear your voice and congratulations!"

It wasn't until almost two weeks later that I was summoned to my Commanding Officer's office once again. "Come in, Meryl," he said when I knocked on his door. He was the only officer who ever called me by my first name, but only when there was nobody else around. We'd flown together on several occasions by the time he called me in, and so he was informal. "I have a surprise for you."

I knew it must have to do with the award, but just waited.

"Looks like you won yourself a month-long trip around the world."

The breath went out of me. I couldn't believe it and I was speechless, a rare thing for me.

"Don't you want to know why?"

I certainly did. I nodded, still mute.

He went on, "Seems that you made an impression on a pilots' association based in Dallas, and they awarded you an around-the-world jaunt."

"But how can I go?" I asked, finding my breath. "I've got training here, and I've already used up two weeks of leave over Christmas in Basic Training." We were entitled to thirty days' leave per year, total. I couldn't see how it was possible for me to go, and I was deflated. This surprise was a dream come true, but it looked like it was, indeed, just a dream.

"Don't worry about it. I've already taken it up with the Base Commander, and we can't let you refuse the award. It would look really bad for the Army, and besides, we feel you earned it. So we've decided to give you Administrative Leave."

"What does that mean, exactly?" I asked.

"It means you're on leave, but it's for business purposes and isn't charged against your ordinary leave. There's just one condition," he said ominously.

"What is it?" I asked suspiciously. I thought I might have to go "paint toilets in the field" first or something.

"You have to *promise* me you'll send me a postcard from every stop." Then he grinned and saluted me—a meaningful gesture in this case, since we were so informal with each other generally.

Numb with the news, I returned the salute. I was stunned at the generosity of it all—being awarded such a huge trip in the first place and the Army's actually letting me take advantage of it in the second place. The public relations people on base called the local newspaper and, once again, my picture appeared on the barracks bulletin board, put there, I think, by one of the women I'd known in boot camp, also at Fort Rucker for controller training. The caption read "Around The World in 25 Days."

And so, for the second time, after having been on a new base for a matter of only a few weeks, I left, this time on a trip around the world. It wasn't an escorted trip, which suited me fine. There were a few formal dinners along the way, in Washington, DC, at the Hilton Towers (where I now lay over frequently as a United pilot) in London and in Paris, but mostly I took advantage of the free travel and went and visited my friends in Austria, France, Germany and Sweden. I came back through India, Singapore, Korea and Japan. Two days in Maui to rest up and get my "beach fix," a quick stop at home in San Diego to say "hi" to my parents and enjoy my mom's cooking, and then a stop in Dallas where I thanked Jim profusely, and took him, his FAA friend Doug and the Marlboro Man out to dinner. Then it was back to Fort Rucker to finish my air traffic control training and begin helicopter school.

It was time to settle down, get serious about my training, and at least pretend I was a soldier. As was so often the case, it didn't quite work out that way.

## CHAPTER 16

# The Guv-nah

Try as I might to become a dedicated soldier after returning from my whirlwind tour of the world, I quickly became restless. Soon enough, I began what I was later to refer to as my "Soldier of Fortune" weekends. I got plenty of flight and travel time through hitching rides, often going wherever the plane happened to be headed.

Sometimes I had a specific destination in mind and didn't care what type aircraft took me there. Other times I'd spot a specific aircraft and went wherever it happened to be going, always trying, and often succeeding, in getting some flight time in the right seat. Many flight crews were quite agreeable to letting me take their place for a while. Usually, the captain was happy to give me some instruction in the various aircraft on which I was a guest. At the very least, I was always allowed to observe, often kneeling in the cockpit for takeoff and landing if no extra seat (known as a "jump seat") was available.

Most pilots were great about giving me rides. It gave them a chance to get in some additional training, and most seemed to enjoy having a new person to talk to. It didn't hurt, either, that I was a female pilot, at that time a true rarity.

Many of the military pilots with whom I hitched rides weren't on any particular mission. They just needed a certain amount of flight time each month to keep current with their requirements. They often didn't care where they went, so I could approach them for a ride wherever I felt like going.

Before long, I'd made a slew of contacts. I could call guys in aviation units from the Air Force, Navy and Marines for rides. For instance, I'd call a C-47 (basically a DC-3) squadron at the Marine Corps Air Station at Cherry Point, North Carolina, and ask if they'd come pick me up on their way somewhere, and almost invariably they would. Or I could call the Navy S-2 (an antisubmarine warfare aircraft) squadron at Pensacola, Florida, and arrange to have them pick me up. I went all over. And I mean *all* over. Nobody said I couldn't, at least not at the time.

A typical weekend would start on Friday afternoon. Fort Rucker is an enormous base, so I'd get a ride from an MP to the front gates. If I got there by four in the afternoon, a U.S. postal truck would give me a lift to the airport in Montgomery. Since no non-postal employees were allowed in the truck, they'd hide me in the bunk in the cab of the truck (under a Confederate flag) when going through weigh stations, and then I'd slip out at the airport.

Once or twice I stayed on all the way to Dallas, but it ate up too much time. On the other hand, I got plenty of rest doing this, as I made good use of that bed in the cab of the truck.

From Montgomery Airport I could hitch a ride on a military or civilian plane all or part of the way to Love Field in Dallas if I was going to fly a trip for Jim, and if not I'd settle for wherever the plane happened to be going, always asking about the possibility of getting some flight time. On the rare occasions when I was unable to sweet-talk my way into actual flight time, at least I was able to observe and increase my knowledge by watching. I was a novelty—a military female and a pilot—and I took advantage of it.

The first time I decided to try to get a ride to Dallas by hitch-hiking on a private plane, the guys at the FBO at Montgomery airport told me I was out of luck. Nobody ever flew to Dallas from there, they told me, or at least it was a rarity.

I was undaunted. "Where's that Jet Commander over there going?" I asked.

"You can't ride on that. It belongs to Governor Wallace. And besides, they're going north, to Minneapolis."

"Why wouldn't I be able to ride on it?" My interest was piqued. They shouldn't have told me I couldn't.

"Because it belongs to Governor Wallace. We just told you. They'd never let you on." Immediately the gauntlet was laid down and I had to see for myself.

I found the pilots of the Jet Commander, told them I was a pilot trying to get some extra flight time, and asked if I could come along.

"You'll have to ask the Governor. He's not here yet, but he should be here any time."

They hadn't said "no" outright and, in fact, were quite friendly. When the Governor's limousine drove up, one of his bodyguards got out first, lifted him out of the car, and placed him in the wheelchair he'd been in since getting shot in 1972, two years before. I seized the moment, awkward as it was, and asked Governor Wallace if I could ride along with them. I had no particular desire to go to Minneapolis, but I wasn't about to let this historic opportunity slip away, either.

I was shocked when the governor, one of the most contro-versial figures in political history, responded, "Why, certainly! I'd be honored if you'd come with us. Any member of the United States Armed Forces is welcome to fly with me anytime! Do you have family in Minneapolis?"

"No, I don't," I said. "I'm a pilot and I've found out that corporate jets will give rides and sometimes give me some flight time. I can't afford to pay for it and I don't know how else to get it."

"Well, hop on! We'll have a chance to talk en-route, and I'll get my boys to give you some flight time to boot!"

And so I flew from Montgomery to Minneapolis with the Governor and his wife, Cornelia, and they both treated me like a family friend. I had my camera with me, fortunately, and asked Mrs. Wallace if she'd take a picture, which she did.

I not only got some flight time in on the way, I flew on the empty airplane back to Montgomery and got some more "stick time" on the way back. When we arrived at Montgomery, the Governor had arranged for one of his staff to meet me with transportation. With the guys at the FBO gawking, to my delight, an official limo picked me up and took me over to Maxwell Air Force base. The weekend was still young so I thought I might as well try to go someplace else.

It didn't occur to me until we got to the front gate of the base what the scene looked like. Everyone on base who saw the governor's limo stopped and saluted, and when I was dropped off at the overnight facilities, I was quickly ushered into the Officers' Quarters, even though, clearly, I was enlisted. I'm not sure exactly what the assumption was regarding my connection with Wallace, but I took full advantage of whatever that assumption was. From then on, I was always given officers' quarters when I overnighted at Maxwell, which I was to do frequently during my time based at Ft. Rucker.

During my travels I often noticed Overseas National Airways' DC-9's. Since they seemed to be everywhere I was, I thought I'd try asking for a ride with them. In Florida I found a couple of crew members at a restaurant with a World War II military theme. All the waitresses dressed in outfits, from "Rosie the Riveter" overalls to uniforms like the one I wore.

"You're ONA pilots, right?"

The two men looked up. "If you want us to be," one of them said, smiling.

The other one said, "We're ready to order."

I rolled my eyes. More often than not, when I went into this particular restaurant, which was a chain with several locations throughout the country, I'd be mistaken for a waitress.

"I'm not your waitress, I'm a pilot." I turned back to the other one and said, "I see your planes everywhere, and I'm looking for a ride back to Alabama." I pointed at my uniform. "Have to get back to base."

"We'd love to take you," said one of the guys, "but we can't."

"Why not?"

"You've got to be an employee. ONA's a contract military carrier. Only civilian couriers can ride."

"But I catch rides on transports all the time."

The guy shrugged and held his hands up in a gesture of apology. "Those're the rules. It doesn't matter that you're in the military. You'd have to actually be employed by ONA as a civilian courier for the military, and that, of course, is not possible while you're in the military."

As always, the words "not possible" immediately put the gears in my brain into motion. "Well, if I *were* a civilian, who does the hiring?" I asked, thinking it would be really something to add this to my growing repertoire of transportation modes.

"We're out of Chicago, so you should go see Bill Bucksman there. He's head of personnel. There's no way he'd hire you, though. At least, not while you're still in the military." As it turned out, they weren't entirely correct.

"Okay, thanks."

The next weekend I got my Marine friends from Cherry Point to give me a ride to Chicago. Even though it was a weekend, I found someone at ONA who put me in contact with Mr. Bucksman on the spot. He turned out to be a terrific guy, jovial and always up for a good joke.

"You came all the way up here for a courier job?" We sat in his office, which was littered with files and miscellaneous papers.

"Yes, I did. It seems like I'd be perfect for a courier job. I'm in the military, so that should be good for security issues. And I'm all over the place all the time, anyway, so why not?"

He gestured to my uniform. "Aren't you kinda busy with that?"

I waved aside the suggestion that my time was governed by the U.S. Military. "Oh, that. Not really. There's plenty of time to fly."

"Well, Meryl, I don't have any openings at the moment," he frowned, "but tell you what. I'll get you authorized anyway, and then, if any openings come up, I'll give you a call. In the meantime, you'll have authorization to fly in our cockpits. I'll put a fax through right now to our dispatch. Technically, you're now in the employ of Overseas National Airways. Whenever you need to go somewhere, just call dispatch, give them your authorization code and employee number, and they'll send an authorization to wherever you are. In just about five minutes, you'll be able to fly on ONA planes wherever they go, whenever you want, anywhere in the world."

"Oh, my God!" I breathed, suddenly intoxicated by the possibilities. "Why in the world would you do that?"

"I have absolutely no idea, but you're young, you're enthusiastic, you took the time and the trouble to come and see me all the way from southern Alabama, for God's sake, and I can't actually think of a good reason why we shouldn't give you rides on our airplanes. It doesn't cost anything, I'm in charge, and I say it's okay! By the way, next time you're in town, let me know and we'll go to lunch. You're buying."

I couldn't believe it, and neither could anyone else. I once made a hundred dollars off an operations guy at Andrews Air Force base where I spotted an ONA airplane. It was headed to Panama City, which was only a little ways south of Ft. Rucker.

"You can't ride on that plane. Nobody can. It's only for civilian couriers."

"A hundred bucks says I get on."

"No way!" he said. "You're on."

"May I borrow your phone?" I asked.

"Certainly," he said, with a smug look.

Within about two minutes after I hung up with the ONA dispatcher, my authorization arrived via fax.

"Wow! How'd you do it?"

"Sorry, that's top secret. And that will be $100, please!"

I was feeling generous, and let him write me a check since he didn't have any cash on hand. I took it and tore it up in front of him, laughing. "Let that be a lesson to you, young man!" I caught my ride home, changing into civilian dress as was required by ONA.

Just before we landed, I changed back into my military uniform. I'd had the pilots ask if there were any helicopters around heading for Ft. Rucker, and as usual, there were. I ran across the ramp from the ONA plane straight to an Army helicopter that had agreed to wait for me. It took the entire short ride up to Ft. Rucker to explain how I'd managed to be on the ONA plane.

Eventually someone at ONA wised up, and my privileges were abruptly terminated about a year later. Although I never got even one minute of "stick time" in the ONA aircraft, they served their purpose as I traveled tens of thousands of miles with them, closing the transportation gap on my Soldier of Fortune weekends.

## CHAPTER 17

## One Mo' Guv-nah

Another weekend, I decided to try and make it home to San Diego for a home-cooked meal. I always carried a carpetbag, made for me by my sister-in-law and, in my dress uniform, I met my customary mail truck outside the main gates at four after air traffic controller class.

The mail carrier dropped me off at Maxwell Air Force base in Montgomery. I'd called ahead and knew they had a flight to Houston that afternoon and I figured I could keep heading west from there until I got to San Diego. After I got on board, however, an Air Force agent came on and asked for a volunteer to disembark. The plane was full and there was a captain who needed to get on board. Since I was just out for the trip on a whim, I volunteered to give up my seat.

"Thank you so much," the operations agent gushed as we made our way back to the terminal. "We've got a flight to Colorado Springs in the morning, if you want to take that."

"Sounds good."

"It's a V.I.P. flight, not listed for general passengers, so putting you on is very hush-hush," he said conspiratorially.

I nodded knowingly, having absolutely no idea what he meant.

"And I'll get you squared away for the night."

"Sounds good," I said again. The agent was in for a surprise with the flurry of attention we got from the staff at the overnight facilities because of my Wallace "connection."

Saturday morning I boarded the flight to Colorado Springs. It was a large aircraft and beautifully appointed. There were couches and reclining chairs everywhere. I sat in a huge leather chair that had a hassock, and there was a telephone mounted on the wall next to me. I put my feet up and vaguely wondered what the deal was with this airplane. It certainly wasn't like any other military transport I'd seen so far.

Seated about the plane was a slew of priests—I half-expected them to cross themselves on takeoff—who were military chaplains. I was so intrigued with the comfortable furnishings that I stayed seated in the passenger cabin on takeoff. Once we reached altitude I made my way to the cockpit.

After introducing myself, I asked about the plane. "So what's the deal on this airplane? Why is it so luxurious?"

The pilots laughed. "Don't you know?"

I shook my head. "No."

"It's a former Air Force One."

"No!"

"Yup. President Johnson's."

"You're kidding."

"Nope! And you know that big leather chair? That was President Johnson's."

"*I'm* sitting there!" I cried. "Hey, does the phone work?" I'd assumed it didn't. This was a long time after Johnson was in office.

"Sure does."

I couldn't believe it. "May I use it?"

"Have at it. The call will go through the White House. They'll route it for you."

"This'll be great." I thanked the crew and went back to the phone. "Hello, may I place a call to San Diego?"

The call was put through, and I could hear everything as my mother answered the phone. "Yes?"

"Hello, this is the White House with a call for Mrs. Getline from Meryl Getline."

"Sure, put her on."

"Mom, *the White House!*"

"So I heard."

"You're not surprised?"

"Meryl, my beloved daughter, I have received calls from you from all over the world: Moscow, Vienna, Tel Aviv, Paris, Berlin —"

"Yeah," I interrupted, "but I'm on a plane!"

"Again, not surprising. Where are you?"

"I'm not sure. Over Louisiana, I think. Mom, you'll never guess! President Johnson used this airplane, and I'm using his phone to call! That's why the call was routed through the White House."

"How'd you manage that one?"

"Oh, you know. Just bumming around. I thought I'd come home for dinner."

"Will you make it?" she asked. "What should we have?"

"Spaghetti, but don't count on it Mom. If I don't make it, I'll try some other time. I've got this flight to Colorado Springs, but nothing lined up after that. I'm just faking it this trip."

"Okay, well, I'll set you a place just in case."

"Thanks, Mom. I love you."

"I love you, too."

At Colorado Springs, I got on a T-29 (military trainer version of a Convair 240) headed for Fresno, California. I made it a point, whenever possible, to be in the cockpit for takeoff and landing. In this case, I had to kneel between the pilot, a six-foot, ten-inch full-blooded Cherokee Indian and the copilot.

Just as we took off, the left engine sputtered and quit. I clearly heard the Indian pilot say, "Uh oh," almost casually, and he put the airplane back down on the runway. "Damn!" He said. "Third airplane this week that's had a problem. Well, we're not going anywhere today, at least not in this airplane."

It was Saturday afternoon, so I knew I wouldn't make it home for dinner that night unless something else came up, but it didn't. Instead, the T-29 pilot and copilot invited me to dinner, where they regaled me with piloting adventures like ones I myself was starting to have.

The next morning, well before dawn, they gave me a ride to Stapleton airport up in Denver. They both had relatives there and were going anyway, since they were stuck waiting for their airplane. I asked them to drop me off at the most expensive-looking FBO. I figured I'd go somewhere fun, and it might be more fun to fly in style—President Johnson's plane had quickly spoiled me. I had of course already called my mom the day before, explaining that I wasn't going to make it after all. She always understood these things.

In front of one FBO I saw a gorgeous four-engine corporate jet. "That's it! Stop the car." I thanked my military pilots and went in search of the civilian pilots who flew this beautiful airplane. They were inside the FBO, called Combs Gates. I didn't know the aircraft type, and found out it was a Lockheed Jetstar owned by Martin Marietta. They were headed first to Fort Dix, New Jersey, and then to Ft. Lauderdale where they would remain for a few days. They got permission to take me along from the executives they were flying that day and then gladly helped me aboard.

As I boarded, the first thing I saw was that the interior was plusher than I knew an airplane could be. The second thing I noticed was that there was an Army General already seated in the plane.

He must have had his own secret, because he avoided my startled stare. It wasn't a common occurrence for generals to be flying around on corporate jets. I saluted as I went by, but he didn't say a word and neither did I. In fact, we did not exchange a single word the entire trip. I silently thanked whatever intuition compelled me to remove my nametag whenever I went off base.

The general got off the plane discretely at Fort Dix, and then we headed to Ft. Lauderdale, where they dropped me off at a particularly lavish FBO called Hangar One.

This FBO had a pool, which was surprising. Their building, it turns out, had originally been intended for an airport motel.

"May I take a swim?" I always carried my swimsuit with me, along with my passport, because you just never knew.

"Sure thing," an employee said.

By this time it was Sunday afternoon, and I had formation at seven the next morning. I was starting to get vaguely uneasy about making it back to base, but I still had time. I just needed to get started. I was not encouraged when the guys at Hangar One told me that most of the traffic from Ft. Lauderdale was northbound, to Atlanta and Washington, D.C., places like that. But they promised to keep a close lookout for me and in the meantime, I went swimming. The guys even brought out some sandwiches for me. I knew people who took vacations more stressful than this!

As I paddled around the pool I started to overhear a heated conversation on the deck across the pool. I paddled a bit closer. Three men were standing close together.

"...Look," one man said. "I'm sorry, but no can do. I'm sick as a dog. You guys are on your own. Take a bus or something. I've got to get some sleep." With that, he headed inside.

The other men just stood there, looking after him. I paddled closer still, and then leaned up out of the pool. "Trying to get somewhere?"

Both men looked up, startled, and then one of them spoke. "Yeah."

"Where you headed?"

"Atlanta. Then west Georgia."

"What are you flying?"

"Beech Baron."

*Nice,* I thought. More than nice—positively providential. Just a few days earlier I'd been invited out on a T-42, a Beech Baron, at Cairns Field at Ft. Rucker, and we'd flown to Atlanta, where I'd made some approaches. It had been my first time in that aircraft, and my first time in Atlanta. The coincidence was almost beyond belief, even to me. "You know, I'm a pilot. I'm current in an Army T-42, which is the same thing as a Beech Baron, and I just flew it to Atlanta a few days ago."

They looked at me quizzically, then at each other, but seemed interested. "You're a pilot?"

I nodded my head. "I'll take you to Atlanta, if you want. But you guys have got to get me back to base no later than seven o'clock tomorrow morning."

"Okay, let's go! We have a function to get to, and we're already late."

Because of their hurry, I didn't bother to change out of my swimsuit. I thanked the guys at Hangar One for their hospitality and wrapped myself in a towel. Their original pilot was still around and feeling just miserable, so instead of giving me a flight check, he simply told me about the plane's various idiosyncrasies. The two men remained inside getting clearance from their insurance to list me as their pilot.

While the pilot was showing me around, I asked, "Who are these guys anyway?"

He looked surprised. "Don't you know who that is?"

"No. Should I?"

"The taller guy is George Busby."

It didn't ring any bells with me.

Noting my blank expression, he said, "*Governor* George Busby, as in Governor of Georgia."

"Oh!" I said. "The only governor I know is George Wallace. I flew with him a couple of weeks ago." Two governors in two weeks. *Wow, what're the odds?*

"*You flew Wallace?*" he asked incredulously.

"Well, I didn't exactly fly him. I flew *with* him. Long story."

We were supposed to be in Atlanta for just two hours, and then, for whatever reason, they were terminating at a strip near a town in western Georgia whose name I no longer remember. By the time we got there it was two in the morning.

Tom, Governor Busby's aide, had called ahead for a limousine, but it wasn't there yet. He insisted on waiting with me until it came. Governor Busby was picked up by somebody else and had already left. "Thanks, Meryl," Tom said when the limo arrived. "You really came through in a crunch."

As I settled back in the spacious car, I replied, "The pleasure was all mine."

The ride back to base on not-that-well-traveled-roads seemed to take forever. Somewhere along the line I had gotten cleaned up and was dressed once again in my Class-A uniform. When we arrived at Fort Rucker I had just about five minutes to formation. Dozens of soldiers were already milling about, including my gruff First Sergeant.

This was starting to get weird—it seemed like I was developing a reputation for arriving at Monday morning formation in a different conveyance each week. One time, it had been a Bekins moving van, another time a fire engine, and still another time a jeep that looked like it was right out of the Beverly Hillbillies. I arranged to be sitting on the back in a rocking chair playing a banjo as we drove up.

I'd never arrived by limo before, and I asked the driver to pull up as close to the group as possible and play along with me. I stepped out of that limo like a starlet at the Oscars. The driver helped me out, and I turned to him and, in a loud and deeply affected British accent, said, "Thank you, James, evah sew much."

To my delight, he bent his head and made a great show of kissing my hand. "Until I once again have the privilege, Miss Getline," he boomed obligingly for my "audience."

And with that, I moved to line up for formation, the performance having the desired effect. My First Sergeant was glaring at me while all the others were looking on with delight at the whole scene.

What can I say? How could I have any self-respect at all if I were to waste an opportunity like that?

## CHAPTER 18

# The Trouble With Camels

A few weeks later I hopped up to Chicago. Bill Bucksman, my friend in personnel at Overseas National Airways, had called me earlier in the week and asked if I wanted to have lunch. Never one to pass up a free lunch, I called the Marines and asked if they could arrange a flight to Chicago Saturday. "Can I bring some friends?"

It happened to be a three-day weekend, which turned out to be fortunate. This was one of those occasions when the Marines had to get in a certain amount of flight hours, but didn't especially care where they went.

I love the Marines! I put up a flyer on my barracks' bulletin board: "Free Trip to Chicago. Leave Saturday, Return Monday. Call Meryl."

I got twelve girls together and we met the Marines at Cairns Army Airfield near Fort Rucker. They picked us up in a C-47—the equivalent of a DC-3. After dropping off two girls in St. Louis, the rest of us flew to Chicago, where we went our separate ways for the weekend.

"Sixteen-hundred hours on Monday," the Marine pilot reminded us. If we missed that flight at four pm it'd be difficult to make it back to base before leave ended.

I found Bill in his office, ready to go.

"Meryl!" he bellowed when I popped my head in the doorway. "Just in time for lunch. Come on." He led the way, not to his car, but out onto the tarmac.

"Where are we going?" I asked.

"Now, if I told you that, it would spoil the surprise."

I thought it was a little peculiar to be getting on a DC-8, but I certainly didn't mind. I had a whole three-day weekend, after all.

Once airborne, we headed east. *Okay*, I thought, *maybe we're headed for New York. That'll be fun.* "So, Bill, where are we going for lunch?"

"Nice try, Meryl, but I'm not telling yet," he smiled mysteriously. "You've got leave for the whole three-day weekend, right?"

"Sure do."

"Good. You'll need it." That gave me pause, but still I didn't know what to make of this announcement.

We flew for hours, far longer than any flight to New York. But he wouldn't tell me where we were going until we landed, an impossibly long flight later.

We landed in Casablanca. Needless to say, I was starving by that point, although there had been some refreshments on board. "Bill, don't you think this is kind of far to go for lunch?"

"Oh, we're just refueling. We haven't got to lunch yet."

"What!"

He offered me no further explanation, and we took off again. My habit of always carrying two items—my bathing suit and my passport, came in handy. Bill already knew I carried my passport because it was required of their couriers for overseas flights, and I was authorized worldwide.

We finally landed in Nairobi. Bill emerged from the plane hitching up his pants, as though we'd just got out of the car at the local Denny's. We took a taxi to a restaurant for "special" burgers.

"Camel burgers!" he announced proudly.

"Bill, did you just drag me halfway around the world for *this*?" It was just a hamburger, made with a hump in the middle as a local joke.

"Good, isn't it?"

I had to admit it was. Mine was a bacon camel burger, to be exact.

I didn't get to see any of the sights in Kenya, because after the burgers we had to fly right back to Chicago, and then I had to hightail it back to base. The aircraft was only on the ground in Kenya for a few hours, long enough to clean (it had been a charter flight with paying passengers), refuel and re-crew. How I envied the pilots who did this for a living!

I barely made the flight back to Cairns and Ft. Rucker. It was late Monday night when we arrived, exhausted, back at base. As we slunk toward my barracks, a voice behind us said in a menacingly singsong tone, "Specialist Getline."

I stopped in my tracks and slowly turned around. The other girls scooted away without looking back. It was my First Sergeant, standing in the shadows. I swallowed and turned around. "Oh, hello," I said, smiling.

"Hello."

Silently, I thought, *Uh-oh! No Coors!* I had gotten into the habit of bringing at least a six-pack or two in my ever-present carpetbag for the First Sergeant from my weekend jaunts whenever possible. However, at that time it was only available west of the Mississippi, which was part of the mystique and attraction. I certainly hadn't gotten any this trip. They didn't have Coors in Chicago, let alone in Africa. "Uh, I didn't get far enough west this time to pick up any Coors."

He looked crestfallen.

"But," I said, "I'll be in Dallas next week and I'll bring back two six-packs next weekend. Okay?" I knew no matter what, I'd better head west next weekend and get the man his fix.

He cheered up at that, and I did keep my promise, keeping relations with him on as even a keel as possible. Lugging Coors beer around in my carpetbag was a small price to pay for my freedom.

It wasn't long after the camel burger trip that I got to Turkey for a weekend. This was on an Air Force C-141, a very large transport. We stopped briefly at Torrejon, Spain, and then continued on to an Air Force base in Turkey. I didn't get a lot of stick time in on this particular flight, but I did get some. I didn't care much, though. It was a thrill to once again be traveling so far abroad.

When we deplaned, the wind was gusting up to about thirty miles per hour. I clapped my hand over my Army "pot hat," sometimes called a "block hat," a sort of bowler hat made out of a reinforced material that felt like cardboard. I made the mistake of letting go, and there went my hat. "Oh, no!" I wasn't nearly quick enough to catch it. A strong gust of wind picked it up and deposited it on the other side of a low, wooden fence bordering the airfield.

There were some people and various types of livestock meandering around. I saw a man with a camel walking toward where my hat lay, and it was clear to me that neither man nor camel noticed my hat lying there. The wind was still blowing, but my hat remained where it was. Maybe the camel would miss it.

There wasn't time to get over the fence. I didn't know a single word in Turkish, but just called out "Hello!" The wind carried my voice away, though, and the man didn't hear me. I tried again. "Sir! Look out for my—" Too late! The camel planted a hoof squarely on top of my hat.

I couldn't tell if it was salvageable or not, so I climbed over the fence, which fortunately wasn't all that high, to go get it and inspect the damage. You know those old movies where some guy takes the other guy's fedora and shoves his hand right through the top? That's pretty much what happened to my hat, except in this case it was the hoof of a camel that nearly separated the top of my hat from the surrounding material. The center part was still attached by a few threads, and I found I could sort of balance it, and it would stay for a little while, anyway.

I was all set to return to the U.S. when I realized I'd managed to enter the country without having my passport stamped. This meant a delay that would keep me from making formation. Resigned, I called base.

"Hello," I warbled to my First Sergeant over the phone I was handed. "I've got a bit of a problem."

"Getline? Where the *hell* are you? You sound like you're halfway around the world!"

I laughed weakly. "Well, funny you should say that…"

When I told him where I was, he practically reached through the phone to grab my neck. "Getline! Do you have *any idea about Army rules?*"

"Well, honestly, no one ever really went over—"

"—You're not supposed to ever, *ever* be more than *thirty miles from base!*" he bellowed. "Do you hear me? Thirty miles!" Funny, he'd never mentioned this before, but I knew why.

I swallowed hard. "Sir, I promise to bring back a whole case of Coors the very next— "

"Get your ass back to base!" he roared, and hung up.

I was able to straighten things out after all and caught my ride home, still barely making it in time for an I.G. (Inspector General) inspection, which was conducted with our things laid out on our beds.

I was still fiddling with my hat, having arrived not even five minutes before, when the I.G. entered with my First Sergeant and the inspection began. I had carefully balanced it so the middle was lined up with the outer part of the hat, but right on cue, it collapsed downward as the Inspector was looking at it, attached only by a thread. "What's that about?"

"Sir, camel got it."

"What kind of camel?"

"A small camel, Sir."

"Small camel? You mean a baby camel?"

"No, Sir, not a baby camel. Maybe a teenager. Just—kind of small."

"Where was this camel?" he asked. My First Sergeant, standing behind the I. G., gave an almost imperceptible shake of the head.

Too late. "Turkey," I said.

"Turkey?"

"Turkey."

"I see. So a teenage camel in Turkey stepped on your hat. May I ask, where was your head at the time?"

I didn't know what he meant at first. "My head was still attached to the rest of me, Sir," I offered.

"Soldier!"

I swallowed hard before replying, "My head was not in the hat when the camel stepped on it, Sir."

"Good, I was beginning to wonder."

The girl next to me could no longer stand it, and snorted as she tried to stifle her laughter. I was so fatigued from the trip that the whole unlikely conversation had taken on a quality that was somewhat surreal.

I was bracing for the reprimand regarding the thirty-mile-from-base-restriction, but it didn't come. I honestly hadn't even known about it. As long as I kept my First Sergeant supplied with Coors, he hadn't bothered to mention it, and certainly nobody else had. Not until Turkey. If I hadn't placed that phone call, I probably would never have known.

The inspector narrowed his eyes briefly. "Well, try to be more careful with your uniform," he said, and then continued down the line.

Later, I saw the Inspection Report with the demerits and type of demerit beside each girl's name. Mine said simply: "Block hat: Camel Damage."

That along with the "monkey facing wrong way in wall locker" was earning me a reputation for the most mentions of wildlife in my Demerit Reports.

The First Sergeant never said a word to me after that inspection other than telling me to get to Supply and get that hat replaced immediately, which I did, although I kept the damaged one for a long time as sort of a trophy. There was not one more word about any thirty-mile restriction. He knew better than to mess with his supplier. The man needed his Coors.

I had done little to endear myself to any of my superior officers, the Coors notwithstanding. It's not that I went out of my way to antagonize them, but my interests didn't exactly coincide with theirs.

I did get some satisfaction, however, from one particular phone call. It was a quiet afternoon. I was hanging about outside after school, making plans to do some flying later that evening with some guys from the helicopter training program.

A soldier came around the corner and stopped when he saw me. "Getline," he panted, clearly out of breath, "First Sergeant's office. He's lookin' for you."

My friends chided me as I headed across the quad to my First Sergeant's office. I had no idea what I'd done this time. Since Turkey I'd been laying low, spending my time flying on local helicopter missions with only occasional forays off base, mostly beer runs to Dallas. We'd go out late at night while everyone else in the barracks was asleep. It was terribly exciting to be out on combat training rides in the middle of the night. At least I knew I was within the thirty-mile radius.

My First Sergeant's office door was open. He stood behind his desk with the receiver in his hand and the most perplexed look on his face. As I walked in, he placed his hand over the mouthpiece and hissed, "Governor *Wallace's* office?"

To hide my surprise, I smiled knowingly and, as I reached across the desk for the receiver said, "Oh, yes, I'd forgotten."

His mouth fell open.

"Yes? This is Meryl. Oh, *George*! How nice to hear from you! How are you?"

I held the mouthpiece away from my lips, looked over my shoulder at my incredulous First Sergeant and gave him a full smile.

"Why is the governor calling you?" he whispered hoarsely.

"I don't know," I whispered, cupping my hand over the phone.

I spoke back into the phone. "Oh, George, I'd love to, but I won't be able to go. Not during the week. I can only go with you on the weekends. But thanks so much! Will you call me again if something comes up? You will? Terrific! Thanks so much!"

I delicately placed the receiver back on the phone base, smiling. My First Sergeant's mouth opened and closed like a fish gasping for water.

I sighed, and said, "He wanted to know if I could take a flight with him day after tomorrow." I neglected to tell him that the gentleman on the other end of the phone was George *Mason*, the personal assistant to the governor whom I'd met on that trip to Minneapolis. I would never have presumed to speak so informally to Governor Wallace. But I wasn't about to dispel the illusion. I positively live for moments like this. The look on his face as I departed his office was worth the whole three years in the Army.

## Chapter 19

## Let's Go to Smokey Joes!

After much agonizing deliberation, I decided not to go into the helicopter training program after all. When I found out pilots in helicopter school were forbidden to fly any fixed-wing aircraft during the entire school, which lasted several months, I decided to skip it. The helicopter time would do nothing to further my flight time as far as the airlines were concerned, and I figured I should be able to free up some time to seek additional fixed-wing time that would help further my career goal.

I'd received lots of flight time in helicopters, but had never learned to hover, arguably the most important and most difficult aspect of helicopter training. Some of my Navy friends had given me instruction on how to hover, using a helipad surrounded on three sides by water in Mobile, Alabama, but it wasn't enough. I knew I wouldn't be able to resist going and getting a helicopter rating, but it would have to be in a civilian helicopter, and it would have to wait. I'd learn to hover then.

So, when I completed air traffic control school in 1975, I transferred to Fort Ord in northern California. It was nice to be back in my home state, at the scenic base just north of the Monterey Peninsula. Better still, it was a fresh start. I would be spending my time working as a controller, and even more time flying.

Two of my three brothers—Scott, the youngest, and Ned, the oldest—lived relatively nearby. Scott was in Pacific Grove, just a few miles south, and Ned was up in Berkeley, not that far away. Ft. Ord also put me within driving distance of San Diego, about eight hours away. My parents and middle brother, Lorin, still lived there, although Lorin had long since moved into his own house.

As soon as I got out to California, I checked into my duty assignment at Fritzsche (pronounced "Fritchy") Army Airfield at Ft. Ord. On the way to the tower my very first day, I stopped in at the civilian flying club and offered my services as a flight instructor. They were extremely glad to have me, as there was a severe shortage of fixed-wing instructors around. Most of the Army pilots were trained only on helicopters, but wanted to learn to fly fixed-wing on the side and would rent planes and take flight instruction at the flying club.

When I first arrived at my new assignment at Fritzsche Tower, no one in the tower knew I was a pilot and flight instructor. I was just another air traffic controller. So there was some surprise, needless to say, when high-ranking officers started coming up to the tower looking for their instructor.

Our tower chief, two floors below, would bellow over the intercom, "Officer on the way up!" and everyone would snap to attention. I, however, would stand about casually, waiting for my student. The first time it happened, the officer in question was a one-star general, coming to confirm his lesson time. I had seen him from the window of the tower cab before he entered the tower and suspected he had a question about his lesson.

"Meryl," General Thompson said, "for the life of me, I can't remember what time our lesson is today. Is it two-thirty or three-thirty?"

"Three-thirty," I said, "but I can always change it. I'm off at two."

"Yeah, if you wouldn't mind, that would be better for me."

"Okay, Mike, see you around two-thirty, okay?"

"Great, thanks." And he left, completely oblivious to, or maybe just ignoring, the salutes around him.

Everyone stood about in mild shock, not understanding what had just happened. "Specialist Getline," the tower chief said suspiciously, "would you mind enlightening us all as to what the hell just happened here? What were you and he talking about?"

"We have a flight lesson today."

"What do you mean, a 'flight lesson'?"

"I'm a flight instructor and he's my student. Well," I corrected myself, "he's *one* of my students."

"Who are your other students?" he asked.

"Well, let's see, there's Captain Brighton, Captain Fellows, Major Martin and....oh, yes, Colonel Stafford."

"But those are all pilots," he protested. "What do they need from you?"

"They're all rotary-wing pilots." I explained. I'm their fixed-wing instructor. None of them is qualified in fixed-wings, so I'm giving them lessons."

The tower chief just sort of gave me a blank stare before asking, "And are we to expect more of these visits?"

"Well, I think it's possible. Do you want me to tell them not to come up?" I asked, concerned.

"No, no. That's all right. Maybe you could just ask them to call first." And he left, while everyone else still stood about, totally shocked. I honestly hadn't given much thought to my high-ranking flight students. They were just my students to me. I can't say I didn't enjoy the whole scene that had just unfolded, though. Talk about first impressions. Three thousand miles from boot camp, and I was still ruffling Army feathers.

After I got settled in as a controller at Fritzsche, it was time to get serious about getting my helicopter rating. Since the civilian helicopter rating had to be gotten in a civilian helicopter, I had to do my training off base although I continued to gain experience flying the Army's helicopters whenever I could get a pilot to give me some stick time.

Astro-Copters, in Oakland, offered a variety of ratings, including helicopters. I did my training in a Bell 47, the type of helicopter used in the television show "M.A.S.H." Since I had to get to Oakland for my lessons, about a hundred miles north of Monterey, I typically got a flying student of mine to take me there or else I hitchhiked a ride on one of Ft. Ord's many helicopters. All of my previous experience had taught me that often the pilots were just trying to get their time in, and were happy to drop me off wherever I needed to go.

After my lesson, I'd get a ride to a base, often Alameda, and stay the night, just for something different. It was always easy enough to call Ft. Ord and either find a solo-qualified fixed-wing student to come pick me up, or an Army helicopter. One or the other always seemed to work out for me.

My helicopter instructor, Barry Lloyd, was a terrific guy, a Vietnam vet who had been shot down while doing his combat tour. Once, during a flight lesson, we flew straight up through a small hole in the overcast. "What if it closes up and we can't get back down?" I asked with concern.

"It won't," was the answer.

Famous last words. Sure enough, the overcast did close up and we were stuck on top of it. Barry was instrument-rated in helicopters, but the helicopter itself was not rated for instrument flying. If we couldn't stay out of the clouds, we couldn't get down. There was nothing else to do but put down near the top of Mt. Diablo, the only piece of land in sight still above the overcast, and walk down, which would take several hours. I refrained from saying, "I told you so."

We left a note inside the windshield of our helicopter on the mountain. PLEASE DO NOT TOUCH THIS HELICOPTER. WILL BE BACK SHORTLY TO PICK UP. "That should do it," he had said, unbuckling his seat belt. "Let's go."

The next morning was a lovely clear day. We got a ride as far up the mountain as we could, then had to make our way the remaining distance on foot up the mountain. The helicopter was still sitting, pretty as you please, in the middle of a meadow near the top of the mountain. The path leading up to it came to a dead end very near where it sat, and there were about fifty hikers milling about as if having come upon some abandoned UFO.

"Excuse us. Pardon us," we said as we made our way through the crowd.

We got in and everyone backed away as we buckled up and took off. I thought I would have to hustle a lift back from Oakland Airport to Fritzsche Airfield and report for work, but Barry flew me all the way back to Monterey Airport by way of apologizing for the whole inconvenience, and I easily caught a ride from there the few miles back to base. (Civilian helicopters were not authorized to land at Ft. Ord without prior permission.)

One day when I was very close to taking my helicopter check ride, Barry and I decided to go buzz my brother Ned's restaurant in nearby Berkeley. Smokey Joe's Café has been there practically forever—more than thirty years—my brother Ned the only owner. It's near the University of California at Berkeley, on Shattuck near Cedar. Some people think by the name that it must be a barbeque place, but it isn't. It's strictly vegetarian, open mostly for breakfast and lunch. As Ned says, it's "where the elite meet to eat no meat."

I had let Ned know I'd be over his restaurant in my helicopter at precisely eleven-fifteen on a Saturday morning. I got a little lost, though, trying to find the right street. We flew pretty low, trying to read the street signs. I'd brought binoculars, hoping I wouldn't need them, but I did. "Barry! Stop jiggling! I can't read the signs! Nope. That's not it. Go two blocks over and one up and I'll see if I recognize anything." Eventually we found the right street, after alerting just about all of Berkeley that we were overhead. We were a little ahead of schedule even after getting lost, but they could hear the racket inside the restaurant and everyone came out to wave.

If ever you're in Berkeley, you might just want to stop by Smokey Joe's and say hello to my brother Ned, the guy with the long hair and dark glasses. He's the guy most likely doing the cooking. You'll still find the picture on his wall that we took from the helicopter that day, looking down on the patrons and owner of Smokey Joe's café. Someone wrote, "You are here" on it as a joke.

Soon after I obtained my helicopter rating, I took a week's leave to go get my ATR, or Airline Transport Rating (now referred to as the ATP or Airline Transport Pilot) practically the day I was eligible, having turned twenty-three and finally having the requisite fifteen hundred hours.

It was very expensive, and without the GI bill I could not have afforded it any more than I could have afforded to get my civilian helicopter rating. There was a misconception that you had to complete your military time to qualify for the G.I. Bill, but somewhere along the way I discovered that you only needed six months of active duty to qualify. An Army official later told me I had the unofficial distinction of having spent the most money the fastest—around $14,000—the full amount available at that time. "Leave it to a woman," he'd added, "to spend the most the fastest."

I took a one-week leave and headed off to Martin Aviation at Orange Country Airport (now John Wayne Airport) in Santa Ana, just south of Los Angeles. I had relatives there and I stayed with them. For my check ride, I had received permission from the Army to land this civilian jet on Army property. We flew up to Ft. Ord and had the distinction of flying the very first jet to ever land at the airfield there. It was a kick. We stopped by the tower and my fellow contollers took turns coming on board for a trip or two around the pattern while I accomplished the various maneuvers required to get the rating.

Along with my Airline Transport Rating, I received my first type-rating—in a Citation, a small corporate jet. It was actually the slowest jet of its type. There was a large fin on the tail, and the joke was it was there to "prevent bird strikes from the rear."

Once back at Ft. Ord I resumed flight instructing, but mostly I flew charters out of Monterey Airport, at Del Monte aviation. There was a myna bird there who said aviation-oriented things, like, "Are you sure you have enough fuel?" or "Did you close your flight plan?"

In 1977, at age 24, I got my helicopter rating. I also got some odd rotary-wing jobs, like flying the "frost patrol." It was my job to fly up and down rows of strawberries in northern California to prevent frost from forming on the plants. Several of us would trade off during the night, stopping at a little restaurant with a helicopter pad nearby for our respective breaks.

Then there was the job taking water samples out of San Francisco bay for one of the plants on the eastern extreme of the bay. I had to get checked out to do it, and the guy assigned to do this thought he'd give me a scare by jerking the helicopter just a little in the same direction I was leaning out to get the water. It did more than scare me. I lost my balance and went right into the drink. It was hard getting out because the pontoon was too thick for me to get a good grasp, on top of which within seconds I was so cold I couldn't feel my hands. The pilot managed to hold the "stick" that controlled the helicopter with his leg and somehow hauled me back on board. He was horrified at what he'd done, but I just chalk stuff like that up to experience. "At least I didn't get killed," tended to be my philosophy regarding these incidents.

Although I was actually making some pretty decent money when I wasn't being an Army air traffic controller, I was always looking for new and enterprising ways to earn more. For example, I opened my "Fly-Through Photo Shop" which lasted about two weeks until I got shut down. There was a catwalk all the way around the tower cab. Guys would hover up to the level of the tower cab, nine floors up, and hover while I took their picture. I tucked my hair up into the baseball-style cap that went with my fatigues, to keep my hair from whipping around in front of the camera lens, and wore my headset so I could communicate with the pilot. "Smile!" I'd say. "Good, good! Now turn a little so I can get a nice profile shot. Okay, one more. *Big smile!* Got it! Okay, stop up in about ten days and I'll show you what we got."

I'd get the pictures blown up and sell them for about $35 apiece, or $80 for a set. It was a big hit and sales were brisk while it lasted, but safety issues were cited and the base commander told me to knock it off.

He was right, of course, and I should have known better. If a helicopter's engine fails at less than a certain altitude, no recovery is possible. The helicopter is going to come straight down and crash. If it's literally just a few feet above the ground, it's survivable. But at ninety feet, which was the height of our tower cab, a loss of power would almost certainly have been fatal.

With enough altitude, which the height of the tower cab did not provide, auto-rotation is possible for a safe landing in the event of engine failure. It's a maneuver you have to be proficient at in order to get rated in a helicopter. As the helicopter falls toward the ground, the rotor will turn faster and produce enough lift so the pilot can maneuver in such a way as to cushion the landing. Hovering at the ninth floor level was just too dangerous. It was fun while it lasted, though, and we got some really good pictures for the guys.

## CHAPTER 20

## The "Good Times" Blimp

You know the feeling you get just before you're run over by a herd of water buffalo? That's the feeling I get every time I think of this story. It was 1977, and I was well into my last year as an Army Air Traffic Controller. Although long-since closed, at the time Fritzsche was one of three linked control towers. The other two were Monterey and Salinas.

All of us in the three towers knew each other personally. We visited each other's towers and even met at picnics and other social gatherings. "JW" over at Monterey was a really nice, good-humored guy named Jim, and "BC" was a curmudgeon over at Salinas.

One night I was on duty in the tower with two other Army controllers. It was a quiet evening. There was little air traffic and the sky was clear and calm. I was working the tower frequency when a call came from the red "squawk box," the hotline that connected Salinas Tower to the east, Fritzsche Tower to the west, and Monterey Tower to the south.

It was BC in Salinas. "Hey Fritzsche, heads-up. The Goodyear Blimp will be calling you in a few minutes—he wants to transit your airspace."

I spoke into the receiver, "General Electric here, thanks." Controllers typically use the first and last letter of their last name as their personal call sign. My last name, being Getline, gave me the initials GE. Since I was military, I thought it funny to call myself General Electric, and once I called myself that, everybody started using it.

Sure enough, a few minutes later, the call came over my headset. "Fritzsche tower, this is the Goodyear Blimp, four miles east. We'd like to transit your airspace en-route to Monterey."

Now, what I should have said, what any normal, responsible person would have said, was simply, "Cleared as requested," and that would have been the end of the story. In fact, there would be no story. But I didn't. Instead, I said, in a sultry voice, "What's it worth to you?"

There was dead silence on the other end, and then a suggestive, deliberately deeper voice responded, "Why, what did you have in mind?"

"Well, you know, I've always wanted to see my name up in *lights*."

The other two controllers in the tower could hear only my side of the conversation, and their ears perked up. One mouthed *What are you doing?* That was Tony, the one who was always so uptight. Already I could see him breaking out in a sweat. The other one, John, just shook his head and grinned.

I put the radio on speaker so they could listen in. The blimp pilot said, with a smile in his voice, "We can do that. That's what we do. So, what's your name?"

I spelled my first and last names and had him read it back. Hey, if you're going to have your name in lights on a blimp flying all over town, you want to make certain it's spelled right.

"Will do. Keep a lookout."

I nodded, pleased with my ingenuity. It might be a quiet night, I thought, but that's no reason for it to be boring. "Say, John, do we have a camera around here?"

"A picture?" Tony whined. "It's not bad enough you're taking liberties with standard phraseology, to put it mildly, but you're going to take a picture of it?"

John called from the closet, where he was looking for a camera. "Oh, get off it, Tony. What's it to you? It's not your name."

"It's the principle of the thing," Tony huffed.

I ignored him and pulled out my binoculars. Off in the distance I could see it coming. As it got closer, I saw it was still displaying advertising. No "MERYL GETLINE" to be seen. The blimp came, and it went, floating by leisurely, like a great, migrating whale, but nothing happened.

Indignant, I keyed the mike. "Hey, where's my name? We had a deal!"

Blimp came back and said nonchalantly, "It'll take a few minutes. The thing's on a computer—it's all automated. The previous program needs to be cleared out while we put your name up."

"Damn," I muttered as the behemoth faded into the distance. Nothing changed as I watched it drift away, and soon enough, not even the binoculars gave me anything. "Forget the camera, John." I was crushed.

I pushed the button on the squawk box and said, "Hey, Monterey Tower, this is General Electric. The Goodyear Blimp is on its way to you, okay?"

Monterey Tower acknowledged, "Okay, General, we'll expect him."

After a moment, I flipped the switch again. "Hey, Monterey, When he gets there, get the binoculars and tell me what it says on the blimp, okay? I'll stand by until he gets close enough."

"Will do," came JW's cheerful answer.

After a few minutes I heard a gasp, and then JW's amazed voice saying, "Oh, my God! How in the world did you manage *that*?"

"What? What does it say?" I asked breathlessly, my fellow controllers at my side, with their mouths hanging open.

Jim said, "It's got your name on it—MERYL GETLINE— in letters thirty feet high!"

I was thrilled. Tony was mortified, and John laughed. "He did it! He really did it!" I shouted to my two colleagues. "I can't *believe* it!"

But then Jim's voice came over the speaker again. "Wait a minute, GE, it says something else, too."

"What? What does it say?" I demanded, still breathless.

"I don't know. I can't quite make it out yet. Too small. Hang on."

"Well, keep your eye on it and let me know right away when you can make it out, okay?" I said, mystified. I couldn't imagine what else the pilot had written along with my name.

"Here we go," Jim said, drawing out each word. "I'm just starting to be able to make it out."

I waited, absolutely breathless with anticipation.

Suddenly there was an explosion of laughter from Jim. It was so loud I had to turn the volume down on the squawk box.

"What!" I cried. "What does it *say*? C'mon, Jim, *tell* me!"

But all I heard was laughter, the teary-eyed, doubled-over type of laughter that cannot be stopped until it's laughed itself out of steam.

Finally, he gathered himself enough to say, through stifled guffaws, "Well, in the *big* letters, you know, the ones thirty feet high, in bright colored lights, it says—MERYL GETLINE. In the little, blinking red lights along the bottom, it says, "FOR A GOOD TIME, CALL!"

Tony sniggered, and John just about fell off his chair, laughing.

"It what?" I squeaked. Gathering a breath, I managed to croak, "You're kidding, right? Please tell me you're kidding."

He kept laughing, and I could make out laughter in the background, too. "No joke. I'll take a picture for ya. You know, for posterity."

He did it on purpose. Blimp waited until he was out of range and then got me. He proceeded to fly all over town, flashing my name in lights for all to see, and there was nothing I could do to stop it.

The next morning, as expected, I got called into my commanding officer's office. "Specialist Getline, has it ever occurred to you to just rent space in my office?"

I said nothing. I was hoping it was a rhetorical question.

"My phone's been ringing off the hook all morning—" he caught himself, and simply said, "You know, I don't even want to know how that happened. Just—"

"Sir," I said, "I really had no idea that—"

"—Getline, is it really too much to ask to have your name in more appropriate places like everyone else, you know, like the bathroom wall?"

I opened my mouth to answer, but he held up his hand. "Dismissed."

"Thank you, Sir," I said meekly, and turned to leave.

As I walked out of his office, I could have sworn I heard him mumble, "No good, anyway, without a number." But I could be wrong.

## Chapter 21

# Buzzard? What Buzzard?

By 1977 I had finished my commitment to the Army. I was a free woman, now 24 years old and impatient to begin my career flying full time. The job market for pilots was still not terrific, and anyway, I needed more multi-engine flight time before I could make applications with commercial airlines. After making exhaustive phone calls to various leads I had, all to no avail as nobody was hiring, I'd heard that a company called IT Corporation down in Torrance, just outside of Los Angeles, might be hiring, so I called them up. IT Corp was a hazardous waste clean-up company, and their corporate plane was a Navajo CR (counter-rotating propellers).

Their Chief Pilot, "Hoppy" Hopkins told me they weren't looking to hire, but invited me down for a visit anyway. Hoppy would prove to be an enormous influence in my life, and someone whom I think about frequently to this day.

"Tell you what," Hoppy said as we sat in his office, "if you want to come on down here, I'll trade you flight time for keeping the plane up."

"Keeping the plane up?"

"Sure, you know, washing it."

I thought about that for a second. Maybe if I did that it would lead to a job at some point. It was the closest thing I'd had to an offer yet. I knew of plenty of other pilots flying for free at that time, with such a scarcity of flying jobs.

"It's free multi-engine flight time, Meryl. It's not a bad deal. And I'll pay you $8 an hour to wash the plane. I usually do it twice a week, and I'll help you."

So, I moved to nearby Long Beach, taking up residence in an old house, and cleaned planes while waiting for an actual piloting job. We flew company executives all over and brought biologists in to analyze spills. Once, when a tanker overturned on the 405—a major Los Angeles freeway that is more often than not really a parking lot—the emergency crews blocked off the freeway and we landed right on it.

Hoppy became my good friend and mentor, instrumental in the ultimate realization of my goal of becoming a commercial pilot. He'd wanted to become a pilot with the majors himself, but years before, while flying a DC-3 for a small airline he'd lost both engines over the Nevada desert and crashed. Although he and his passengers survived, his career as a commercial pilot did not, as a result of the serious injuries he sustained. Instead, he became Chief Pilot for IT Corporation and had been with them ever since.

It was Hoppy who put me on to my next job with Baja Cortez Airlines in Los Angeles, but I continued to fly with IT Corporation after I took that job. About the time I started to fly for Baja Cortez, IT Corporation started paying me as a pilot as well as for washing their airplane. I wanted to fly seven days a week until I reached my destination: an airline job.

Baja Cortez Airlines was a very small commuter based at Los Angeles International Airport, which was a very big deal to me in itself. It seemed I kept edging closer and closer to my goal. Being amidst all the big airlines was exciting.

The gentleman who started Baja Cortez was a former Senior Vice-President for TWA. He was a good friend of the

Chief Pilot, Western Division for Pan Am, and our office was situated in the Pan Am building on the southeast part of the airport. We were right down the hall from Pan Am, and the minute I learned this I marched right in and asked if I could speak with the local Chief Pilot.

His name was Bill Erkes, and he was well known by many of the Pan Am pilots I was to later fly with after United Airlines picked up some of Pan Am's international routes along with some of their pilots. Bill couldn't have been nicer and let me know that he would have gotten me a formal interview on the spot if he could, but Pan Am had a whole slew of laid off pilots and it wasn't going to get better any time soon.

Bill had a real home elsewhere, but when he was in Los Angles he used an apartment for his local crash pad. It happened to be right next door to the apartment I'd rented after I'd moved out of the house in Long Beach. Sometimes we would swim together in the evening and talk aviation. I was never even to interview with Pan Am, so deep was their furlough, but I valued my friendship with Bill, who helped me prepare for other airline interviews.

Because of the friendship between the owner of Baja Cortez and the Chief Pilot for Pan Am, we parked right on the ramp with Pan Am, usually under the wing of one of their 747's. The giant 747 right next to the small twin looked for all the world like a mama and her baby. Baja Cortez used Navajo Chieftains, a slightly larger but very similar aircraft to what I was flying already at IT Corporation with Hoppy.

Surprisingly, I didn't get any static at all from the Chief Pilot of Baja Cortez Airlines, a nice enough guy named Jim who seemed to actually like the idea of hiring a female pilot. If there was resentment among the other pilots, it was not apparent. By then I had several hundred hours of experience in Navajos thanks to Hoppy.

Baja Cortez's routes consisted of a few cities on the mainland of Mexico, primarily Guaymas, where we would usually start our day. Our schedule sometimes had us sitting around as many as four hours in Guaymas, which was often tedious because the temperature typically hovered in the 90's.

We didn't want to leave our airplanes unlocked for fear of vandalism, so we locked them up tight. By the time we were ready to go again, the airplane seemed hot as an oven—so hot that we'd have to take towels and ice to cool down the controls.

One day, on a whim, I brought a cookie sheet and a roll of Pillsbury Chocolate Chip Cookie Dough. When we went inside, I left a batch of cookies in the "oven," balanced on the top of the instrument panel with the sun beating in.

By the time we were ready to leave again, we had fresh-baked-sort-of-homemade chocolate chip cookies! Of course, it was so hot that they weren't actually all that appealing, but it was the principle of the thing, and they got eaten later. In fact, the popularity of my bakery encouraged me to bake more.

After Guaymas, we'd shoot across the Gulf of California over to Baja California, landing most often in Loreto and Mulege, both popular fishing spots. Our stops were based on our bookings. If nobody had made a reservation at a particular place, then we wouldn't make the stop.

Of all the skuzzy places I'd ever landed, Mulege took the cake—a short, often muddy dirt strip with a garbage dump on what was usually the approach end. With the dump came turkey buzzards, enormous, ugly birds with huge curved beaks. Whenever we had to land or take off from there we had to do the best we could to hold off if there was a large group of birds congregating off the end of the runway—a potentially serious hazard.

One day, the coast seemed clear and I came on in for landing. I had a passenger up front in the right seat next to me. I saw the turkey buzzard for about a split second right before he smashed into the windshield, breaking the right-hand side and sending shards from the window right into my passenger's face, which proceeded to bleed profusely.

My side of the windshield was intact, but so covered with blood, feathers and gore I couldn't see through it at all. There was nothing to do but turn the aircraft sideways, take a peek at the runway, and come on in to land while peering the best I could through all the gore. I didn't want to mess around with a second approach with my passenger in such bad shape. I just cut the power and put the airplane down.

Mulege was too little a place for a tower. In fact, there was nothing there at all except a very small motel right on the field. We never even got fuel there, but brought enough in with us to make it to back to the States.

There was one phone available, but I couldn't get the call to go through. The line would fill with static, and then quit altogether. The Mexican running the small motel just shrugged apologetically and said, "Sometimes work—sometimes not." I guess this time, not.

My passenger was improving slightly. We kept bottled water in the airplane and he allowed me to wash his wound to get a good look. It actually wasn't as bad as it could have been—I was afraid of an eye injury, but there was none. But we both knew he needed a doctor and probably some stitches. I got on the airplane's radio and searched about until I found a plane flying nearby with a pilot willing to come and pick up my passenger, who by then was pretty much holding his own face together with a towel from the airport motel.

I felt really horrible for him, of course, but let him know I thought his best bet would be to let this other pilot get him back to the U.S. for medical treatment. He agreed, and told me he

did not hold me responsible. "I may sue the buzzard, though,"
he laughed weakly.

He wrote to the company about a month later, thanking me
for seeing him on his way to medical help, and I was of course
extremely grateful to the other pilot, an American with his own
plane, in Baja California on a fishing trip, just passing by on his
way home.

The next thing on the agenda was to get to a phone and see
what was to be done about the windshield. I looked around and
saw no cars, not even any bicycles. What I saw was a lone
burro.

I asked the man at the motel desk, "Señor, is there any way
to get a car here so I can get to town, or can somebody get me
to town?"

"No, Señorita, no car come. You take burro."

*Terrific*, I thought. "How far to nearest phone?" I asked

"About three mile, Señorita. Take one hour."

And so, with all the dignity I could muster, and still in my
uniform, I got on a burro named "Pepe," who was anything but,
and headed down the one road. Pepe and I stopped at points of
interest along the way—of interest to him, that is, not to me—
my pleadings to hurry ignored completely. There was no question at all as to who was in charge.

Eventually, not after one hour but closer to two, I got to a
phone that actually worked and called the company. They
would arrange for a new windshield, but it would take a few
days, and was I willing to stay with the airplane while I waited?

Yes, I was willing, and Pepe and I headed back to the airport. It started to rain on the way back, and as we plodded
through the mud I began to question my career choice. "So this
is what it's like to be in aviation," I mused aloud to Pepe, who
seemed seriously disinterested.

I wasn't really questioning my career choice. I never allowed my goal to waver, no matter what. If "making it" meant riding on a burro named Pepe in Mexico in the rain, then that's just the way it was going to have to be. As always, I tried to be philosophical about it.

Back at the airport, I got a room at the motel, which, despite its location was picturesque, if somewhat cold and damp. It looked pretty but smelled just terrible, especially when I placed my uniform near the heater to dry.

Apparently Pepe was not up on his hygiene, nor had he been groomed lately—if ever—and I spent hours picking burro hairs out of my uniform when it finally did dry. I was trying to imagine the conversation I was to have with my dry cleaner.

Five torturous days later, after my windshield and an installer showed up, I passed through the international checkpoint at Tijuana. The inspector, one of many I got to know well because of my frequent flights, pointed to the top of the plane's nose. There was a big dent, which was to be hammered out once I got home. "Señorita, what happened there?" he asked.

"I got hit by a turkey buzzard down in Mulege," I said.

A few minutes later while I was still standing around on the ramp waiting for my paperwork to clear, I heard a second inspector ask the first if he knew what had happened to my airplane.

"Buzzard trouble," he said gravely.

"Ahhh," the other nodded knowingly.

Having friends in customs turned out to be not only beneficial, but also life saving, or at least, career-saving. Since we flew people to and from Mexico, we always took precautions to check out the passengers. The last thing the company—and we pilots—wanted was to be flying drugs across the border. But even with the checks, we still sternly lectured our passengers about not taking drugs on the plane. "You will be caught," I'd say, "and if you're caught, not only are *you* going to jail for a very long time, but so am I. The pilot is held equally responsible. So, *do not bring drugs on this plane!"*

Before leaving Mexico, I always gave my passengers a chance to unload any illicit goods they might have. Occasionally, someone would ask for their bag and disappear for a few minutes inside the terminal. I would wait and I didn't ask any questions.

One idiotic trio brought drugs on the plane, anyway. The drug-sniffing dog in Tucson, Arizona, one of our border-crossing stations, caught the contraband, of course, and the plane was swarmed with customs officers. They dragged my passengers out of the plane. Fortunately, they knew me well enough to know I wasn't involved and did not detain me—but not before I'd practically had a heart attack over the discovery. It wasn't the first time in my career, or the last, I was to say to myself, "Well there goes my airline career." This was definitely one of those times.

"I'm so sorry," I said to the customs officers as we stood outside the plane. "I warned all of them. You know I always do, right?" I looked to the other passengers. "Did I warn you guys or not?"

"Yes, you did," they answered practically in unison. They looked appropriately terrified.

"Did I tell you the sniffer-dogs are never wrong?"

"Yes, you did," they answered, as though we were at some weird prayer meeting.

The customs guys said, "Don't worry about it. Nothing you can do sometimes." Thank God. That could have been the end of my future airline career right then and there. "Arrested for flying drugs from Mexico into the United States" is not something I could afford on my resumé.

As the officers led the guys away in handcuffs I shouted after them, "You're going to jail, jerks! *Mexican* jail!" The location of the jail was not Mexico, of course, but I thought I saw them shrivel a bit as they heard it. I was really angry at the jeopardy they'd put us in—me in particular.

This was not the only problem passenger I had during my tenure at Baja. I also had a heckler who, along with his wife, I was to take to Mexico on vacation. I went to pick the couple up in Tucson, along with some other passengers, and he wisecracked as they boarded, wisecracked as they got settled and continued to wisecrack as I was trying to give my safety brief. His wife was mute, completely stony-eyed, probably long ago having given up on having a husband instead of a self-absorbed, unfunny dolt.

I asked him several times to please be quiet and pay attention, but he continued to chatter away loudly, making stupid jokes about women pilots and preventing me from giving my safety brief to the other passengers, who were looking increasingly annoyed. Finally, I warned him. "Sir, if you refuse to allow me to do my safety briefing, I'm going to throw you right off this airplane. Do you think you can put a lid on it? If I can't give this safety brief, then I'm in violation of Federal Aviation Regulations."

But the idiot just wouldn't shut up. I looked at his wife. She looked at me. I unbuckled my belt and went back to his seat. "Sir, you'll have to get off," I demanded, and opened the aircraft door. "I'm serious." I pointed my thumb over my shoulder. "Out of the plane. Please don't make me get a police escort."

He just sat there, looking flabbergasted. "You have *got* to be kidding!"

"Nope."

"I promise I'll be good."

"Too late. You had your chance and I don't trust you to behave later on even if you decided to shut up now. Out!"

"I'll have your job!" he blurted out angrily.

"I doubt it," I replied calmly.

In a huff, he unbuckled himself and got out of the plane. Then, glaring at me, he said to his wife, "Come on, Maureen. Let's go. We'll get there some other way."

Maureen sat, immovable.

"Maureen, did you hear me? Come *on*."

Maureen was a statue.

I folded my arms. "I think Maureen's going on vacation."

He blinked, and opened his mouth, but nothing came out. He blinked again, and then walked away, the rest of the passengers clapping as he left, even Maureen. A couple of days later, I got a postcard from her at the Baja Cortez office. It said, "Wish you were here…glad he is not! Ha-Ha." The postcard pictured a woman lounging on a white sand beach, looking out over crystal-clear water.

Sometimes I missed having passengers, even the obnoxious ones. It was, after all, my dream to fly people everywhere. One day I flew an empty airplane all day, and not a single passenger showed up at any of the stops. No-shows weren't unusual, but it was very unusual to fly such a long day and have absolutely nobody be where they were supposed to be.

I had a special stop to make that day, at a strip near Scammons Lagoon in Baja California. The lagoon is the southern point of migration as well as the breeding ground for the California Gray Whales, who start in Alaska each year on their remarkable journey.

I was to pick up a biologist on that gorgeous day. When I arrived, however, no one was there. This was a firm appointment, and I just didn't want to take off for home without being very certain he wasn't coming, so I took off and flew over the lagoon, looking for him along the way.

The whole area was devoid of human life. What I did see, however, were more whales than I'd ever seen in my life—hundreds upon hundreds of them. There, over the lagoon that day, I had my own private whale-watching experience. It was both awe-inspiring and unforgettable.

I flew overhead for about twenty minutes, decided this guy wasn't going to show, and flew back to Los Angeles. He had in fact cancelled his pick-up, but there was no way for my company to get word to me once I'd left for Mexico.

My day without a single passenger turned out to be one of the most memorable flights of my life, the sight of the congregation of hundreds of whales at Scammons Lagoon burned forever into my memory.

## CHAPTER 22

# A Change in the Wind

Before and during my time with Baja Cortez, I started inter-viewing with some of the airlines. They were just starting to hire again for the first time in years, and were starting to hire women. I had some good experiences, such as the promise of a future interview with the Pan Am Chief Pilot, but also a couple of really rotten ones.

For example, I interviewed with Flying Tigers. Pilots in those days, and maybe even still, went for interviews wearing blue suits. I was no exception, and recall being pleased that my landlord, a sweet older lady, told me I looked "stunning." *Good,* I thought, *qualified and put together,* and I set off for my inter-view feeling confident about my prospects.

This particular interview with Flying Tigers was a prelimi-nary one conducted by some guy in Personnel. Mr. Smith—not his real name—was a short, rotund man who met me with a smile and ushered me into his office. He arranged two chairs opposite each other and offered me a seat. The chairs were on little wheels, and I sort of rolled away when I say down. "Whoa, I've gotchya," he said smiling, and pulled me back.

He moved to his desk, picked up a folder, and sat down oppo-site me. "Impressive," he said, and then looked up. "I can get you in to see the Chief Pilot tomorrow." Pushing off suddenly, he rolled right next to me and, all in one movement, put his hand matter-of-factly in my crotch. "Just have dinner with me tonight," he cooed.

Looking him straight in the eye, I removed his hand from my lap, got up, and said, "I don't want to fly cargo enough to have dinner with you." With that, I turned on my heel and walked out.

I made it as far as my apartment before bursting into tears. My landlord came over to ask me how my interview had gone and found me a wreck, curled up on my sofa.

"Sue the bastard!" she shouted.

"I don't want to, I just want to work," I sobbed. I never wanted a job I'd have to sue to get, and I certainly wouldn't want to work for a company that had people like that in charge of the hiring. I was devastated. I knew if I filed a complaint, it would be my word against his, and it just wasn't worth it.

Though I went through most of my early years relatively unscathed by smarmy men, there were times when some were too friendly because I was a female, or too unfriendly for the same reason. Typically, I made a point to ignore unwanted attention because I was not looking for a date; I was looking to fly. I can say, however, that most of my encounters with men, both as friends and colleagues, were wonderful. Being treated as an equal, simply as a pilot, was always what I wanted.

Among the numerous experiences of sex discrimination, most were ridiculous. For example, while in the Army, I'd heard that a private company called O'Connor Corporation, based in Texas, had an opening for a copilot for their Hawker-Sidley jets. I applied, writing a letter explaining that men, sterling creatures that they are, are not the only creatures who can fly.

The letter got a big laugh out of the Chief Pilot, who in fact gave me a check-ride in the jet when they were in the neighborhood.

Unfortunately, O'Connor, owner of the corporation, did not approve of my gender as a pilot and not only told me I wasn't hired, but was going to fire his Chief Pilot for even considering a woman. It was upsetting to know I wasn't hired because I was female, but it was hardly surprising. When the Chief Pilot told me, I wrote a letter to O'Connor saying it was a big mix-up, and that I'd never been offered the job. This gesture, once again, impressed the Chief Pilot, and we continued to exchange letters, forming a nice friendship from a difficult situation.

But really, next to the snub by the Air Force and the incident at Flying Tigers, most of the events were small potatoes. There was only one other incident that was as upsetting as the day I found out the Air Force wouldn't let me in.

I had been called to interview with United when I was just out of the Army, in 1977. I can't even begin to describe the elation when I received my invitation and First Class ticket in the mail. "Elation" doesn't even come close. I was to fly on a B-747 from Los Angeles to Chicago for the interview. I had never actually flown on a 747 before and was stunned at how big it really was. I was also amazed at the gentleness of the landing. "Like a butterfly landing on hot coals," an expression I would learn later in my career.

Once I actually got to the interview, however, all my hopes were dashed in a heartbreaking moment. When I walked into the interview at United's luxurious corporate headquarters, a panel of five men sitting at a long conference table looked at me in confusion.

An assistant introduced me, saying with an odd tone to his voice that I didn't understand, "Gentlemen, this is Meryl Getline."

I smiled and stood there, hand extended, waiting for them to lean over the table to shake it. "It's a thrill to be here," I said.

They all just sat there staring at me. Finally, one of the suits in the middle said, "What are *you* doing here?"

"I – I beg your pardon?"

He shook his head. "What are you *doing* here?" Then he turned to the rest of the others and they all started whispering really loudly—but not loud enough for me to hear.

"Gentlemen," I said, but they continued their fervent conference as if I wasn't there. I tried again. "*Gentlemen!*" I practically shouted. "You *invited* me, remember?" They all abruptly stopped talking and faced me.

"No, we didn't," another man replied derisively.

"Look, here's my invitation letter," I said hurriedly, thrusting the letter across the desk. I held it there, waiting for someone to look at it.

Nobody was interested in seeing it, but I was insistent. "Look," I pointed at it, "it says right here, United Airlines Executive Offices. Here's the time and the date. Look!"

Another man put on a pair of half-rimmed glass and reached over and snatched the paper from my hand. "Let me see that."

"It must be a mistake," the first man said dismissively. "We don't hire women."

"But how can you say that?" I was utterly incredulous. "It says right there that I'm female." I leaned over the desk to point at the letter. "See right here, where I checked the little box?"

The reading glasses man turned away so I couldn't touch my letter. "Yes," he said over his shoulder accusingly, "but it also says you're a U.S. Army Vietnam era veteran with helicopter time and an Airline Transport Rating. That sounds like a *man*."

I just shook my head, dumbfounded.

"Naturally, we assumed you were male. With your name— Meryl—we missed the "female" part. Nothing about your application suggested you were a female."

"But I checked the box—"

The first man interrupted me and said condescendingly, "Yes, we've just been through that, haven't we?"

"But I'm here," I stammered, "and I'm qualified. Why won't you let me do this interview?"

It was already over. A small man at the end of the table looked at me with something I took to be pity and said, "The public isn't ready for a woman pilot."

I couldn't believe it, and to this day there are some who might not believe that someone at United Airlines told me that, but they did, as had Delta before them a few years earlier. Their personnel director informed me that Delta was a "southern gentlemen's airline" and that they would "nevah, evah, hire any woman as a pilot." The fact is, Delta did start to hire women not long after that statement was made to me in early 1973, but I didn't even know it for several years. By 1977, many of the majors had hired their first women pilots, and United hired their first woman just a few months after my rejection. Of course I tried to get another interview, but was told I'd have to wait the mandatory one year before reapplying, regardless of the circumstances. No amount of arguing would change United's mind.

At different points in my career I vowed to make myself the most qualified pilot out there so no one could refuse me. This was one of those points, and it made no difference. My initial disbelief and humiliation turned quickly into anger and indignation. I reached across the table and grabbed my letter out of Four-Eyes' hand faster than he could blink, and then looked each and every one of those men in the eye. I was seething. "How do you *know* the public isn't ready? Maybe they should *get* ready, because we're here! What do you think, that I'm the only one out there? American, Frontier and Delta—they've

ALL started hiring women! What's the matter with United that you haven't yet?

They sat there, mute, and just shook their heads. I left without another word, so angry, frustrated and disillusioned I couldn't bear it. Everybody who'd ever told me I'd never make it, being a woman, was now in my head saying, "I told you so. You can fly, but you'll never fly for the majors. They'll never, ever hire a woman." These words kept echoing in my head, even though women were now being accepted by many of the majors. Maybe I would still fall short.

I was angry all right, and suddenly afraid. What if I couldn't do it? There was nothing to force companies to hire women, not yet. There were those around me who said I should sue, but, as I'd said before, I didn't want to have to sue an airline for the privilege of working for them.

As it happened, a lawsuit had already been filed, unbeknownst to me, by a minority group against the airlines, and when I was invited to that first interview at United it had been won but was under appeal. The appeal was later lost, and the door at United was suddenly opened to minorities and to women. Too late for me that time around, but United was soon to hire its first women. Those women were furloughed soon thereafter, and several years would go by before they were back at United. In the meantime, most if not all of the other majors were starting to hire women pilots, on at least a limited basis, for the first time in history.

## CHAPTER 23

# Iran

Baja Cortez Airlines was really just a part-time job. They operated only about four days a week, as I recall. There was a con-
siderable amount of flight time involved, since each flying day
was really long. But I still had some free days when I wasn't
flying to Mexico with Baja Cortez or with Hoppy. I needed to
fill that time with more flying.

One or two of the other pilots at Baja Cortez were flying the
rest of the time with a small commuter based at Brackett Field
in Pomona, east of Los Angeles, called Inland Empire Airlines.
They, too, flew Chieftains, and when I became aware of their
existence I high-tailed it out there and presented myself for a
job interview. Although not without some trepidation, they
hired their first woman pilot—me.

Inland decided to expand operations and began shopping
around for planes. Dick Maple, Inland's Chief Pilot, had at one
time been a captain flying 727's for Iran Air out of Teheran but
had left along with other Americans after the revolution. He'd
started calling contacts he had all over the world, including
some in Iran. One friend there, a pilot originally from Peru,
named Luis Michaels, flew for a regional carrier there called
"Pars Air," short for "Persian Air Service." Luis told Dick that
there were three Navajos for sale at $80,000 apiece. This was an

astonishing sum, considering that these planes typically sold for $250,000. *Each!*

Dick started making a deal for three planes, unbeknownst to me, because he knew I'd want to go with him to pick up whatever planes were bought. In fact *all sixteen* Inland Empire pilots wanted to go, and were already nagging him, but my reputation was established enough for Dick to withhold this information from me in particular so I wouldn't have the chance to get at him. I finally did find out about the deal, and ran into him at Los Angeles International Airport during a turnaround.

As I was walking up the ramp I spotted him ahead of me. "Dick! Hey, Dick, wait up!"

He stopped short at the sound of my voice, but didn't turn around, and then kept on going. He knew I was on to him.

"Dick, hang on!" I caught up and grabbed onto his shirt-sleeve.

He kept walking but looked over at me with a forced smile and shouted, "Hiya, Meryl. What's up?"

747's and DC-10's were screaming around us, starting up, taxiing in and out. I kept tugging at his shirt, yelling, "Dick, I gotta go. I *have* to go." I clutched his arm, about to launch into my time-perfected harangue when a few other Inland pilots came toward us and waved hello. Dick stopped to greet them and shook loose of me. "Meryl, get *away* from me, will you?"

We all said our hellos and then the other guys started in on Dick about going to Iran. He was surrounded. "Dick, we gotta go!" we all shouted above the roar and din of jet engines.

Dick held up his hands in defense, yelling, "*Everybody* get away from me!" He turned away and walked inside, away from the noise. We followed like he was the Pied Piper. "Listen," he said sternly, facing us. We had lined up behind him, practically panting with anticipation. "I can't take all of you. You know that. And if I can't take all of you, *none* of you goes." We all stared at him, waiting for the *right* answer, not this one. "Now, go away. Don't you all have planes to fly?"

With that he walked away, and we were left to think about other tactics. Dick was immovable; wheedling and nagging weren't going to work. Since I have never been one to be deterred, and since I likely had more experience finding unusual ways to get what I want than did my colleagues, I set about figuring out how to get to Iran. Once there, Dick couldn't turn me away, and would have to let me fly back with him. He shouldn't have even considered doing this alone, and I convinced myself it was my *responsibility* to see that he didn't.

I called the Iranian Consulate in San Francisco to see about getting a visa. I was disappointed to learn that none were being issued; Dick's work visa was still current, since he'd worked there recently. For three days I sulked, and then called the consulate again. I spoke with the same man who'd told me they weren't issuing new visas, and began to work my wiles on him.

This time I told him the details of my trip, embellishing only a little. "Listen, my boss needs two people. It's better to fly with two people over the North Atlantic, even in two planes. You don't want this guy flying alone, do you? I mean," I lowered my voice conspiratorially, "he's no spring chicken."

Dick was only in his forties. And people fly solo across the North Atlantic all the time, but I had to make my case as strong as possible to get the attaché to give in.

There was silence on the other end. Finally, he said, "All right. Come up and we will discuss this matter further."

Just a few hours later, I was in the cockpit of a PSA (Pacific Southwest Airlines) jet to San Francisco. Small as Inland Empire Airlines was, our administration people were really good at negotiating reciprocal cockpit privileges for our pilots with an amazing number of air carriers, including PSA.

I was prepared to go through my whole story again, to wear down whoever was to hear my plea. But when I arrived, the attaché said simply, "Come, we will process you." He led me down a long hallway. As we walked, he said offhandedly, "I need a passport-size photo. Did you bring one?"

"No, I didn't know I'd need one! Is there someplace around here where I can get one in a hurry?" This was downtown San Francisco, but it was also getting quite late in the day.

"No," he said. "Our office is closing in a half hour and there isn't time. You will need to come back."

I couldn't come back! Or, at least, I had no desire to come back. I was already picturing arguing with someone else who again would tell me it was "not possible" to issue me a visa with the current political situation in Iran, while this guy was out sick that day, or transferred, or whatever. No, I had to do this right now. There was also the fact that I had no idea when Dick was actually planning to leave. He wasn't discussing his travel plans with anyone—least of all us pilots.

I frantically looked through my purse. My Mexican work visa! It was required to fly for Baja Cortez Airlines into Mexico.

"Will this work?" I asked him, holding my breath.

"Yes," he said, looking at it, "this will do nicely."

The picture was so firmly attached to the visa that I had to pretty much destroy the Mexican visa to get it off. I knew I'd have some explaining to do to the Mexicans next time I saw them, but at least I had my Iranian visa. For the moment, it was, "Goodbye, Mexico!" and "Hello, Iran!" I thanked the nice Iranian diplomat and had one foot out the door when I heard, "Stop right there, please."

*Uh-Oh!* I thought. *This can't be good.*

"There is something I must know," he said.

"Yes?"

"Is it possible that you can explain to me why it is that I've had over a dozen phone calls in the last two weeks, all from young-sounding men wanting to apply for an Iranian visa, just as you did?"

I explained it to him the best I could, the fact that we were all pilots, all headed for the airlines, hopefully, all in search of some new and different flying experiences. The lure of the adventure of flying airplanes halfway around the world was too much to resist.

"Ahhh!" he said. "I think I understand a little better."

"And now may I ask *you* a question?"

He nodded.

"Why did you issue this to me when you turned everyone else down? You did turn them all down, right?"

"Yes," he answered. "I issued one visa only—to you—for several reasons. You sounded interesting and intense. I've never heard of a female pilot, but you had urgency and insistence in your voice, and, oh yes, there was one other thing."

"What was that?" I asked, intrigued.

"You called back," he said, and shrugged his shoulders ever so slightly.

"I called back..." I echoed.

"Yes, out of the dozen or so phone calls I received, you're the only one who called back. I was actually hoping you would not so easily accept "no" for an answer after I had a chance to think about your request. I wish you a pleasant and safe journey."

Unbelievable. As I caught a bus back to San Francisco airport, so I could once again get a ride on PSA down to Los Angeles and report for my evening flight to Las Vegas, I mused about the way of the world. *I called back.* That was the deciding factor between my success and the failure of the others.

Being a female pilot had added to the intrigue on the part of the Iranian diplomat, but once again, it was the persistence of the request that made the difference in the end.

Back in Los Angeles, I kept flying as if nothing had changed, as if Dick's dictate was the final word. The next step, and the tricky part, was to put a trace of sorts on Dick. My plan was to find out his complete travel plans and then follow him. Dick's secretary, knowing all us pilots well, knew we'd be looking for information. Naturally, she shut up like a clam, refusing to give out any of Dick's itinerary. What I did learn was that the only thing holding up his trip was a shipment of Jeppesen world charts that hadn't yet arrived. You have to order them specifically, and they're also very expensive—needless to say, Dick couldn't leave without them.

I approached my Pan Am friend, Bill Erkes about the best route to take from Teheran to Los Angeles. If anyone could give me advice on this, he could. He responded with, "Well, let's go and see!" and next thing I knew he and I were sitting in the cockpit of a parked Pan Am 747, charts spread out between us. My preference was to go the long way around, flying east from Teheran over the Orient. We charted the course in both directions, just to be sure. I wasn't sure what Dick was planning, as he'd refused to have any discussion at all with his pilots about it.

I found Dick in his office soon thereafter, my Iranian visa tucked away in my pocket. I wasn't going to let that little beauty go anywhere I couldn't reach out and touch it. "Dick," I smiled, standing in his doorway. "I hear you're waiting on charts."

He sat at his desk, looking over documents, and without looking up, simply grunted, "Uh-huh." There couldn't possibly be anything so absorbing that he couldn't look at me; I knew he was doing his best to avoid making eye contact.

"I can have your world charts by tonight," I said coyly, "if you'd like."

He looked up at that. "How?"

"Well, Dick, being the ex-military woman that I am, I have ways."

"What kind of ways?"

"I'll just go get the ones you need from the nearest base. I have friends," I said nonchalantly. "They're not the same as the Jepps (Jeppesen Charts) you ordered, but they're certainly adequate. You can let the Jepps catch up with you later."

"How soon could you get them?" he asked.

"Today, from Norton Air Force base, right here in Los Angeles."

"Okay."

"Okay?"

"Okay."

"*Okay!*"

"But that's it, Getline," he wagged his finger at me.

I bolted out of his doorway, hearing him yell after me, "Just the maps, Meryl! Just the maps, which you're handing over to *me* who is going *alone* to Iran…"

Off I went to Norton and told them what I needed. They showed me to a storeroom and said, "Help yourself." I looked around. The whole world was pretty much covered. I took some time and gathered up every chart I could possibly imagine that might be needed. Military charts lacked the detail of the Jeppesen's for which Dick was waiting, but they were free, they were adequate, and they were mine.

Charts in hand, I headed back to the office. But in a flash of inspiration, I pulled over to find a phone, and called Meg, his secretary.

"Hullo, Meg," I beamed into the phone.

"Hi, Meryl," she responded warily.

"So, I've got Dick's charts."

"Uh-huh."

"But they're going to expire right in the middle of his trip, you know, so I have to know his exact travel plans because I need to get him the new ones as soon as they come out."

She bought it! Then again, I was good. *Really* good. Meg gave me his itinerary starting from the moment he left his front door. And I had to know his every move so that I wouldn't lose him along the way. For all I knew he could take a detour for some reason and then I wouldn't be able to find him.

At the same time, I didn't want him to know I was there before we arrived in Iran so that he couldn't send me home. Meg told me he was to fly on Freddie Laker's Skytrain, a DC-10, to London, where he was planning a three-day layover, and then on to Iran on Iran Air. It was perfect. If he got on the front of the DC-10 in Los Angeles I'd get on the back, and vice versa. I could *hide* on that plane.

Our reciprocal rights with Freddie's was for free tickets; there was only a tiny service charge. The whole thing would cost me just $10 round-trip from Los Angeles to London! I'd worry about getting from London to Teheran later.

There was a major glitch, however, when Dick quit the company about three days before the trip. He'd had one too many disagreements with the management and said he'd had enough. At first I was despondent. *There goes my trip to Iran. All that work for nothing.* But then I thought he might un-quit. He'd quit in the past but always come back. This was something like his fourth time, so I decided to wait it out and see if he came back.

He didn't. Finally I called him at home on a Sunday afternoon. We chatted amiably for a few minutes, and then I couldn't take it anymore.

"All right, Dick, let's cut to the chase. What are you going to do about the airplanes?"

"Well, the deal's off."

"But you could make a fortune off those planes!"

"Don't remind me, okay? I don't have the capital. The company was putting up the money. Where am I supposed to find $240,000, let alone on such short notice?"

"You can't pass this up! The payoff's too huge."

"What part of 'don't remind me' was hard for you?" he snapped, irritated most likely as much by the bad timing of quitting as much as my reiterating the painfully obvious.

"Okay, I'll call you right back."

"Um, okay."

We hung up. I had very little time, and much to do. I called Channing Clark, a friend introduced to me by Hoppy. I wasn't sure how wealthy he was, but, even though he lived modestly, I had my suspicions. Hoppy'd told me he had retired early when he hit it big in the stock market.

Chan's claim to fame was being an "Aerial Yachtsman." This self-bestowed title referred to the fact that he owned and flew the only Fleetwings Seabird in the world, an amphibious aircraft he jokingly referred to as the "SST"—Stainless-Steel Tub. It's a remarkable aircraft, built in 1936, and flown by Howard Hughes at one time.

Chan had let me fly it with him on several occasions. His was the only one left of the six that were built. I believe all the others crashed. It was so unusual looking, that pretty much whenever he flew it somewhere, someone would call the local newspaper; he was famous in his own right. He later helped make a movie for the Smithsonian Institute. Filmed in part at Glacier National Park in Montana, I saw the film myself on a visit to the Smithsonian years later. Chan and his SST also appeared in several television shows and commercials.

Whenever I would fly with him, he'd say to be sure and let him know if I ever needed help with anything. So I did. "Chan, remember what you said to me a while back?"

"Certainly, Meryl. What do you need?"

"I need a loan." He was probably thinking I needed something like twenty bucks.

"Sure, how much?"

"$100,000." I figured I'd start high so we could negotiate.

There was dead silence on the other end.

"Chan? Chan! Are you there?"

"You've got to be kidding."

"No. I can explain." So I told him that we'd buy one plane, sell it at a profit, and then go back for another, and so on until we'd bought everything we wanted and made a nice profit. I made it all up as I talked, having no idea what I was going to say next. But it sure seemed to make sense, and it *was* a terrific deal. Best of all, Chan loved a good story, and this one was good. "Chan, can't you just picture the cocktail parties? You'll have them eating out of your hand with this one."

I could feel him thinking on the other end.

"Besides, it's no risk to you. We'll put the money in a secure account in London and use it for collateral until we sell the plane. Your money won't be at risk while we try and make the deal come together."

Now I could hear him breathing. "It sounds like something I could do," he said slowly. "I'd have to sell some stock."

"Let me have Dick call you. He's been putting the deal together."

I called Dick back. "I got the money."

He burst out laughing. "It's Sunday afternoon. I just got off the damn phone with you. How do you have the money?"

Indeed, it had been exactly seven and a half minutes since we'd hung up. I'd timed it. I don't know why. I think I was

trying to judge my own negotiating skills. "Just call my friend
Chan. He's ready." I gave Dick the number. "Oh, tell him it's a
hundred, not eighty."

"A hundred…?"

"Thousand. Up front, for the first airplane, which we'll
come back and sell before we go and get the next one," I said,
as if it should have been obvious to him.

We hung up and he didn't call me back. Forty-five minutes
passed. By then I was just about frothing at the mouth with anx-
iety. I started calling Dick, but the line was busy, so I paced
around my apartment. A few minutes later, Dick finally called.

"We're on! I can't believe you talked him into even listening!"

"Great!" I was jubilant. "When are we leaving?"

"We? *I'm* leaving. Where the hell do you think you're
going?"

"It was *my* idea!" I laughed. "Of course I'm going."

"Well, you can't go anyway. You don't have a visa."

"Yes I do."

"Wha—Wha —"

"I've got it in my hand as we speak."

"How?" he asked vaguely.

I knew he was defeated. "Dick, after everything, do you
really need to ask?"

"No," he sighed, "I suppose not. What were you going to do
if I hadn't quit, follow me?"

"Yup."

In the spring of 1979, just a few months before the
American hostages were to be taken, we got everything together and set off for London. We spent three days in London, during which time Dick was arranging his pass on Iran Air as a former employee. I intended to buy a reduced-fare ticket for
myself.

In the meantime, however, he became ill; an ulcer flared up big-time. He wasn't going to be going anywhere for a while. Lying in pain in his hotel bed, he told me just to hang on. "Just a few days," he said weakly.

I paced the room. "Dick, it's been three days already. And on top of that there've been delays getting this far. I need to go on and get things started before somebody else snaps up those planes."

He propped himself up on his elbows, his arms shaking from weakness. "You shouldn't go alone."

"Dick," I complained, "I'm not a child; I've been all over the world. I can handle this. Besides," I put my hands on my hips, "you're not in any condition to be my chaperone if I did need one."

He collapsed back on his pillows. "You're right," he said reluctantly, "Okay, go on."

I went on without him, finding a free ride in the cockpit of British Airways instead of buying the reduced fare on Iran Air. Being a pilot, even for such a tiny airline, certainly had its advantages. I had no idea how "real" passengers managed with the limited flexibility and expense of regular airline tickets. Just as when I'd been in the military, I knew I could get anywhere in the world for nothing or next-to-nothing.

Dick and I agreed to meet up in about a week. Luis, Dick's friend from Peru, picked me up at the airport. Dick had planned to draw up the contract when we arrived in Iran, so I had nothing written when I got there—Dick was too ill to write a draft; it was up to me to figure something out.

After picking me up, Luis decided to take me out to dinner. "*Not* Iranian food," he declared emphatically. Although I thought it bizarre at the time, since he was living and working there, I learned later that he really, *really* didn't like Iranians.

I was still recovering from the ride from the airport into Teheran when Luis mentioned dinner. Practically the first thing I saw was a newly slaughtered sheep at a stand selling meat. The blood was being drained into the gutter right on the street. I gagged as we drove by, trying to avert my eyes.

I wouldn't have even known it was a restaurant we were entering if Luis hadn't told me. The building was unmarked, on a dark, dingy street. We had to knock on the door to be let in, and once inside, the door was quickly locked behind us. It reminded me of the scene in my favorite novel *Catch-22* where Yossarian, the main character, is walking down a similarly oppressive street in Rome. He sees a sign that says, "Tony's restaurant. Fine food and drink. Keep out."

Of all things, it was a Japanese restaurant. I'm not big on Japanese food, and ordered a small steak. It was okay, but when I saw the tab I almost fainted. The equivalent of $90! Luis had ordered some fish that, frankly, looked a little scary. There were no side dishes, either, or bread, or anything like that. Certainly there was no alcohol involved; even carbonated drinks were illegal, although the soft-drink "Bubble-Up" was to be legalized within the month. We drank bottled water. Luis's only remark was that it was typical for a small dinner to cost that much, and insisted on paying the entire amount.

Finally, I got to the hotel and sat down at a typewriter where I drew up an agonizingly simple five-sentence statement—my idea of an Agreement to Purchase. I had absolutely no concept of what such a document should look like, so I just made it up as I wrote it, worrying that both it and I might just possibly be laughed right out of the country.

I also dropped the price down a couple thousand dollars apiece on the condition we'd buy all three planes, figuring this would give us room to negotiate in our favor. At the end of the document I typed, "Mr. Maple and I would like to assure you of our good faith and wish only the best of relationships to enhance our future business dealings with you and Pars Air." Satisfied that it was the best I could come up with, I decided it was time for a swim.

Though I'd seen women covered head to toe in traditional *chadors* as Luis took me from the airport to the hotel, I didn't think there would be a problem with my swimming in the hotel pool. The hotel was a Sheraton, after all. I was wrong. My first day in Teheran, I was arrested. *Dick will be pleased*, was my first thought as I was unceremoniously hauled out of the swimming pool by three Iranian policemen doubling as security guards for the hotel. They told me I was under arrest. It didn't seem possible that I was in trouble already. I hadn't yet been there twenty-four hours.

Fortunately, all I got was a stern lecture not to do it again. Women were not to use the hotel pool, let alone swim with so little clothing on. It was for men only. I got the message and never swam again until that day at the Caspian Sea with my Iranian friend, Toba, where I was not to fare much better.

While waiting for Dick to arrive, I was allowed to fly as a guest copilot for Pars Air and even drew a small salary. This was the company with the planes for sale and for whom Luis was a pilot. We flew passengers around the country in F-28's, which are somewhat similar to DC-9's. The planes held about sixty-five passengers, and often we had something like fifty-three people and twelve goats. The smell was just terrible and I wondered what compelling reason there was for goats to travel so much, anyway. I never did find out.

On one trip, we had a Pars Air manager with us in the cockpit, observing. We were just taking off from Mehrebad Airport in Teheran, and below us were about forty airplanes. The escort leaned over my shoulder and pointed. "Meryl, do you see those airplanes down there?"

"Yes."

"You can have them all. They're all for sale, and we'll give you a very good price for them."

I laughed. "You're kidding." These planes had belonged to the Shah before he was deposed. "Even the 707?" It had a gold bathtub. I'd been taken on a tour of it a few days before. I couldn't imagine it would be for sale, let alone that we could ever afford it.

"Yes, even that."

Out of curiosity I asked, "How much for just the 707?"

"$8,000,000."

Not a bad price, but I felt I was getting in a little deep here and knew I had to wait for Dick.

A few days later, Luis picked me up and we returned to the airport, this time heading straight for an extra large hangar. Inside, we were met by three men in military uniforms who showed us the planes. They were in very good condition with no obvious defects. I was allowed to fly each in turn in order to complete the inspection. Dick and I had discussed stopping in London to have them retro-fitted with extra fuel tanks for the long flight home. Even going the "short" way, over the North-Atlantic, we would need them.

The president of Pars Air was waiting for us when we returned from the last test flight. I handed over the sales document I'd written, and after he'd looked it over, it was handed back to me with a positive nod. No argument, no attempt at negotiating the price back up. Nothing.

I looked at Luis, wide-eyed, questioning the cheap price tag the Iranians had agreed to so easily. I had negotiated a price of $74,950 apiece on the condition we bought all three. We all—

Dick, Luis and I—later concluded that they must have been the Shah's personal property. Now deposed and in exile, there simply was nobody around to protect what had been his property. No wonder the planes were so cheap and the new government so willing to do business with us.

The terms agreed to, we had a contract drawn up and ready for signature when Dick arrived. He had finally recovered and made it to Teheran, but when he did, our agreement with the Iranians started to break down. Our deal had to go through Iran's Central Bank. Things dragged on and on, and we couldn't get a straight answer about completing the transaction. Khomeni's regime was blamed and no one seemed to have any idea why they were holding up our deal. Eventually, Dick had to leave and go back to London for more medication or something, leaving me in Iran—in limbo. I had the strangest feeling when he left that he wasn't coming back. I was right.

The next phone call I got from Dick was from Los Angeles.

"Meryl, how's it coming?"

"Same as before you left. When are you coming back?"

Silence.

"Dick?"

"I'm not, Meryl."

"What!"

"It's crazy, I can't deal with those people. You finish it off, you were doing just fine without me." I hoped I was imagining that he sounded just slightly miffed.

"You're kidding. Please tell me you're kidding." This was unbelievable. He had just up and left me with completing the deal. No warning, no nothing.

"When you're ready to ferry the planes out, I'll come back. Just let me know. Stay as long as you have to, to finish the deal."

I was dumbstruck, and hung up the phone. *What else can I do*, I thought, *but try to finish the deal and get the hell home?* In Dick's absence, however, nothing changed. At first I was determined to see it through, but after a while, Dick started calling, saying it was time to drop it and come on home. He didn't think Khomeni's minions were going to let the deal happen.

What Dick didn't know, and, for that matter, what I didn't know was that the F-28's I was flying were actually on lease to the Iranians from the Fokker Aircraft factory in Holland. As I hung out in Teheran, I learned from two Dutch officials and a Dutch mechanic who were there, also staying at the Sheraton, that they had come to Teheran to try and get at least some payment on the planes for which the Iranians had never actually paid anything at all in the two years they'd been on lease.

One night the three Dutchmen invited me to join them for dinner at the hotel. The conversation started out inconsequentially enough, then suddenly took an unexpected turn.

"We know you fly with Luis. We know Luis hates Iranians. How do you feel about them?"

I had no idea where they were going with this. "Well, I can't say I'm thrilled at this point. I've been here for weeks, have accomplished nothing, it looks like my deal isn't ever going to be approved, and I may as well accept defeat and go home."

"Good!" One of them said.

"Here's the thing," another said. "We want our airplanes back. They're not paying for them and they're not going to."

I waited for someone to continue. They seemed to expect something from me. "Well, I said, what are you going to do about it?"

"We're going to confiscate them."

"Confiscate them? How?"

"With your help, hopefully."

"Okay, you just lost me. What does this have to do with me?" I asked, genuinely perplexed. I wasn't following this conversation at all.

"We want you to fly one of our airplanes back to Holland."

I was incredulous. "You mean *steal* it?"

"No," the first one who had spoken said calmly. "Not steal. *Confiscate*. The airplanes belong to Holland. Iran has stolen them from *us*."

"Why don't you fly your own pilots in to take them back?" I asked, still confused about why they were discussing this with me.

"Because they wouldn't have the access to the planes that you do. You fly for them anyway—you and Luis."

"Well, I don't think Luis is a good candidate for this. He's been here a long time now. He wouldn't want to burn his bridges here."

I was completely caught off guard by their next statement. "Luis has already agreed to help fly one of the airplanes out. He has had enough and is ready to leave Iran for good."

I sat there, stunned. More than stunned. My brain was whirling. Suddenly, it started getting funny. Dangerous, but funny. "So the Iranians are flying your airplanes for free, you're mad and want them back. Does that pretty well sum it up?"

"Yes, that's it. Will you think about it?"

I didn't need to think about it. It got more intriguing by the second. I decided to go for drama. "No," I said. "I won't think about it."

All three men just looked at me, not knowing what to say next. I let them stew for just a moment or two, thinking I'd refused, before saying, "I don't need to think about it. I'll do it!" It sounded like fun.

And we sealed the deal there at the table at the Sheraton, clinking our glasses together in a toast, our glasses filled with newly legalized Bubble-Up. What a country!

A few days later, our plan was finalized. Luis would take one plane, and I the other. Although normally flown with two pilots, one could handle it. We'd take off and just appear as if we were on a normal flight. Pars Air often did charters as well as regular runs, and hopefully nobody would think anything of it. We'd file a normal flight plan, but just keep going. We'd meet later when we stopped en-route to Holland for more fuel.

We also gathered about twelve Iranians who wanted to flee the country. No sense in flying an empty airplane. It was getting bigger and bigger.

I started carrying my packed carpetbag with me to the airport every day so it wouldn't seem suspicious having it. I'd already developed a good relationship with people at the airport, and since Luis was a well-known pilot for Pars Air, he was already above suspicion.

The night we were supposed to pull off the repossession and escape, however, more guards were posted in and around the airport. Tensions were already high in Iran—it was only a matter of days before the American hostage crisis would occur— and security was notched up every day. The next night was worse. Even in my hotel there were shootouts between the new fundamentalist government and people trying to smuggle liquor into the country. I was crushed, as were the Dutch and as was Luis. We had no choice but to give up the plan. It was a terrible failure all around, as I knew I had to abandon the Navajos, too.

I left Iran and a few days later, Luis did, too. In fact, he wound up a pilot for Inland Empire. Chan got his money back from London where it had been placed in escrow, and even though there was no happy ending, at least he would have a terrific story to tell.

I quickly got over the fact that Dick had bailed out on me, and was actually glad for the excitement that ensued because of his absence. I don't know whether he'd have considered the Dutch proposal for himself—knowing Dick, he very well might have—but I do think he would have tried to protect me by blocking my own participation.

It wasn't long before I was back home, telling Chan all that had happened, and flying once again for Inland Empire airlines. Things there were about to change, however.

## CHAPTER 24

## My Own Private Hollywood Bowl

There is a story I heard recently that resonates with my own experience as a pilot—except for the glitter. Liberace, before he was famous, was playing in little bars and nightclubs. But he had bigger plans. Realizing he was wonderfully talented and should be playing to thousands in huge concert halls, Liberace rented the Hollywood Bowl.

There, in that storied amphitheater under the Los Angeles stars, Liberace held his first big-venue concert. For two hours he played his heart out, and then he gave two encores. And through it all, there was nobody there to hear his virtuosity but the people who worked there and whoever else may have heard the sounds in the night air.

A scant two years later, Liberace was at the piano again, in the open shell of the Hollywood Bowl. Only this time, the Bowl was packed, and the people loved him. He played his encores to actual thunderous applause.

This story has always intrigued me because I pulled my own "Liberace" in aviation. Like him, I had a crystal clear goal for myself and, in striving to realize it, found myself actually creating it somewhat before its time.

Before I was a pilot for a major airline, I was able to fly in the left seat—the captain's position—of a United Airlines DC-10. I rented the jumbo jet for myself from the airline for which

I wanted to fly, United, just like Liberace rented the Hollywood Bowl for himself because it was one of the venues where he wanted to play. There was a saying at the time: "What's the best airline job in the world?" The answer was, "*Any* airline job." Although it was true, my ultimate goal was always to fly for United.

I had no illusions about the difficulty of what I was trying to do, but my whole life has been spent moving forward—going around, over, or through obstacles in my way, but always forward.

After I returned from Iran, Inland Empire moved its base of operations twice: once to Los Angeles International and then up to Fresno, with a second base in Visalia, just south of Fresno. Since Inland was by now providing the bulk of my flight time, most of it in their recently acquired turboprop Metroliners, I chose to move with the company, leaving Hoppy, Baja Cortez and an assortment of other odd flying jobs behind. Baja Cortez was to cease operations shortly after I left, but I continued to see Hoppy occasionally when he passed through Fresno on a corporate run—Chan, too, whenever he was in the neighborhood with his Seabird.

The pilots of Inland Empire Airlines—almost without exception—were just trying to build flight time until we could get picked up by one of the major airlines. The terrific thing about it was that the airline's management knew this, openly acknowledged it, and even supported our goals. We didn't have to sneak around like pilots with other commuters, secretly going to job interviews, or go to some flight school or other for extra ratings while trying to prevent the company from finding out about it.

In those days, the route to a job for a major airline started with a flight engineer's rating. A flight engineer is the crewmember in the cockpit that sits sideways in airplanes such as the B-727 and DC-8, which were designed for three pilots.

Back then, the fuel, hydraulic, air conditioning and other systems were located separately on a side panel and handled by the flight engineer, who also figured out various takeoff and landing speeds, flap configurations and other computations.

The pilots had it relatively easy—all they did was fly the airplane. In fact, the copilot's position was, at one time, known as "early retirement," as they reportedly did so little. The flight engineer worked much harder. It was sometimes laughingly referred to it as the "valet station," since it was also the job of the engineer, or "plumber," as they were also called, to hand up beverages, hang coats and so forth.

These days, aircraft are made for just two pilots, and so, at least in the U.S., there has been the virtual elimination of the flight engineer or second officer position. The copilot—in fact both pilots—have absorbed what the flight engineer used to do. However, modern aircraft are much more sophisticated and automated, so that helps keep the workload under control.

Some airlines, including United at one time, had professional engineers who were not pilots, but later, for the most part, the flight engineer, or "Second Officer" position, was just something you had to do on your way to being allowed to fly for a commercial airline. Without a flight engineer's rating, you could all but forget about getting an airline job. Although I'd interviewed with some airlines without the rating, I knew all along that my next step toward becoming a commercial airline pilot was to get that flight engineer's rating.

There was one hitch: it was expensive to obtain. Unlike many jobs, there is no on-the-job training for pilots, and back then there were few flight schools. Certainly regular colleges and universities didn't offer degrees in airline piloting. The Air Force and Navy had always been feeders to the commercial airlines. The rest of us had to pay for everything.

And what a proposition that was. For a flight engineer rating, usually obtained in a Boeing 727, you had to expect to pay at least $2,000. The few existing flight schools were expensive, as were those airlines that offered flight training. After calling around to a variety of places, I found to my surprise that United Airlines' program was the most financially flexible—and I wanted to take advantage of that flexibility.

The others, a private flight school in Burbank, California; Boeing in Seattle; Braniff and American in Dallas also offered flight engineer training in the B-727, but were immovable in the pricing to get that training. Interestingly enough, later in my career I had occasion to train at all of these facilities: Braniff (B-727 flight engineer training), Boeing and also Western Airlines (B-737 type-rating), American Airlines (B-727 type-rating), and then of course United Airlines after I got hired with them.

About the same time I was setting my sights on the flight engineer rating, I heard that some guys I knew were going out and buying training for other type-ratings—the most popular being the Boeing 737. The ones doing this often were using their G.I. Bill money. Mine was already used up, though, most of it having been spent on my Airline Transport and Citation Type-Ratings.

I knew a B-737 type-rating was also a big plus for getting hired. You can fly as a copilot in one of these jets with a few hours' training, but to be a captain you had to be "typed." The airlines liked pilots who were already typed because, as one often heard at the time, the airlines were hiring captains—which meant they wouldn't have to pour tons of money into training and then find out later you couldn't cut it when it came to being captain because you couldn't pass the very stringent check ride required for a type-rating.

The cost at that time for a B-737 type-rating was around $10,000 and took several hours of training in a jet, simulator, or both. The check ride was done in an actual B-737 jet. Later, as simulators got more sophisticated, it became possible to become fully type-rated in certain jets without ever flying the real thing, but at that time actual airplane time was still required for the check ride.

I really wanted the B-737 type-rating as well, but I didn't have enough money for both that and an engineer's rating. So I reluctantly made up my mind to go just for the flight engineer's rating, which was required by many air carriers. Although a type-rating was desirable, it was not actually required by the majority of carriers.

As a born negotiator—at least, I like to think so—I looked forward to bartering with the guys at United for a better deal on training time. One afternoon I flew from Los Angeles to the United Airlines Flight Training Center in Denver and met with a really sweet sales guy named Buddy. He proved to be instrumental in getting me where I wanted to go.

I sat in his office and got straight to business. "What can we do about the cost, Buddy? I need to do this, but I can't afford to pay full price. Can't you give me an airline discount or something?" I asked lightly. "What about a 747? What kind of price could you get on a flight engineer's rating for that?"

Buddy was mild in both appearance and manner, probably in his late forties or early fifties. He leaned back in his chair. "Well, Meryl, let's see what we can do."

"I know you'll give me the best possible price," I smiled as he reached for the phone.

And he did. Not only did he work with me to get a really good deal on the engineer's rating, he also negotiated a flight engineer's rating for me in a DC-10 for the cost of what others were paying for a B-727 engineer's rating, a much smaller jet. United didn't have a 747 simulator available at the time for outside contract training, as it turned out. But I gladly settled for the DC-10, stunned at the low price I was getting.

I beamed. "Wow, Buddy!" I never expected this! A DC-10, really?"

He said, "I'm giving you the simulator pretty much at cost. I know you want this really, really badly."

"I know I can't afford it, but what kind of price could you get me on a DC-10 type-rating?"

A thin layer of sweat beads appeared along his thinning hairline. "Meryl, it's about $4,000 an hour. You'd have to have the minimum five hours in the actual airplane, the same as United pilots."

Well, that was certainly out of the question.

More calls were made, and shortly thereafter a United Airlines DC-10 Fleet Captain "happened" by. He shook my hand firmly.

"So, you're looking for a dual rating?"

"Yes, but I can't afford $4,000 an hour."

"You know," he put his hands in his pocket, forcing himself into a casual stance, as if he was about to offer me some fatherly advice, "at your experience level, it'd be a mistake and a waste of money anyway."

"Waste of money? How?"

"Well, you don't want to spend all that money and not get the type."

*What do you a mean, 'not get the type!'* My blood was starting to boil. I hated being played, and I hated it even more when someone thought they could do it to me. "Why wouldn't I get the type?" I asked archly.

"Come on, now," his tone was folksy. "You don't have the experience—"

I cut him off. "Give me a break. I'm an experienced commuter captain, and you know as well as I do that a plane is a plane."

The fact was I couldn't afford the rating anyway, but I really resented the negative attitude. Buddy later apologized to me, but I wasn't blaming him. He had my gratitude for arranging the DC-10 flight engineer rating for me.

I headed back to California and Inland Empire to ask for a month of unpaid leave so I could get my flight engineer rating.

"Denied," the business manager, Joe, told me.

"What!" I was incredulous. How could they deny unpaid leave? There were plenty of pilots who could fill in for me. "How could they? Call them again!" I reached for the phone, but Joe was smiling at me.

"Just what is so funny? This is my *life* here!"

"I said they denied your unpaid leave request. I didn't say they'd deny a leave."

"What? How?"

"*Paid* leave. We're going to keep you on full salary for the month you're gone."

"What! Why in the world would you pay me to go train somewhere else for a rating I can't possibly use here?"

"Listen. Think of the credibility. We get to tell our passengers that some of our pilots are trained at the majors. We all know you're going to bail this job at some point, but we'll still get some mileage out of this in the meantime."

Indeed, they did. Later, there were several articles about my unusual rating, both in the local newspaper and in Inland Empire's *Inflight Magazine*. In addition, an ABC news affiliate came and did a story about it. We used a United Airlines DC-10 parked at San Francisco to tape the story of my DC-10 rating.

The night the story ran, I was flying from Fresno to Los Angeles, and several controllers asked along the way if I was the one on the evening news. There were so few women flying commercially at that time that it was almost a given that it had to be me, and of course it was. The story was later picked up nationally.

"Oh," Joe said as I was leaving. "Dale's going with you. Okay?" Dale Tregoning was Inland Empire's current chief pilot. "He wants his engineer rating, too."

This was unexpected but welcome news. "Great!" Suddenly, everything was, indeed, great again. I'd not only nabbed a great training deal, but I also obtained a training partner. I was so excited by all this good fortune I almost couldn't stand it.

Dale and I drove together to Denver, stopping in beautiful Yosemite National Park along the way. There were other stops, and it struck me that I'd never really driven cross-country. I'd been all over the world by now, but I'd never seen much of the United States from the ground.

In Denver, we stayed in a private house with some friends near United's training center, and Dale and I started ground school. Because there is no piloting involved with being a flight engineer, we were to do all of our training in the simulator.

Although these days some simulators may be used in lieu of airplanes for ratings, at that time the FAA required the use of a real airplane for the actual check ride, even for the engineer's rating. Since you couldn't feel pressure changes in a simulator, you had to go up in a jet, where manual pressurization could be practiced.

Our FAA inspector, Tommy Thompson, called it "spinning the wheel." Manual pressurization, to be used only if all three of the other pressurization systems failed, involved spinning a yellow wheel to open and close the pressurization outflow valve. It was a little tricky to keep up with it. Even doing it correctly, you could feel the pressure changes when Tommy disabled the automatic pressurization system during the check ride.

Somewhere during training, it started to seriously bug me that I was learning exactly the same stuff the pilots of these jets had to learn, but wouldn't be able to fly the actual jet because of the expense. United had told me at my original meeting with Buddy that flight training would have to be done in the airplane. At $4,000 per hour, with five hours minimum required, I couldn't afford it. Not even close.

I contacted the FAA in Denver and asked to meet with them. They came over to United one day after ground school and I asked them why I'd have to train in an airplane for a type-rating. Why couldn't I just train in the simulator?

The FAA said I could! It was just *United's* policy for their own pilots to let them have a few hours of experience in an actual airplane before taking their FAA check ride. As far as the FAA was concerned it wasn't required. Since I wasn't with United their policy didn't apply to me.

All that was required was that the check ride itself be done in a real DC-10 since there were no simulators yet certified to replace the airplane for a type-rating check ride. Those would come several years later, and with them the need for training in a real airplane was eliminated. Pilots would, of course, still have a training check airman accompany them on their first several flights.

So I went back to the negotiating table and asked how long it would take to get me up to speed flying the DC-10 as a pilot. After all, I was an experienced pilot. With Inland Empire, along with flying our scheduled routes I'd been flying Metroliners on tours through the Grand Canyon, flying below the rim, still legal in the late seventies. The Metroliner was fast and a bit unwieldy. If I could manage something akin to a *Star Wars* flight battle sequence, surely I could handle the highly sophisticated DC-10. When I finally got into the DC-10, it was, as I'd suspected, much easier to fly than the Metroliner. The DC-10 is a wonderful, responsive aircraft. I wasn't in the least intimidated by it, although I was in awe of the fact that I was training in it. You could say it was love at first flight.

I renegotiated my deal so that, after flight engineer school on certain days I would get some flight training in the simulator—left seat, which is the captain's seat and where one sits to get type-rated. It's the command position. The right seat is for the copilot or sometimes for an instructor, depending upon the situation.

United gave me an initial evaluation and we decided that four hours of simulator training would be ample. There was a new ground trainer that United actually had me test for them, and they asked for my feedback on its usefulness. It was a computer-based program, called PLATO, I believe, although I no longer remember what the acronym stood for. The program allowed a pilot to sit in United's library and touch a screen to simulate the type of commands used in the airplane for different phases of flight. It was free for me to use, very effective, and United did go on to use it for its own pilots. The purpose was to save time needed in the simulator, which was expensive to operate.

By the time I got into the simulator, all that was left to do was to get the feeling of flying such a large jet. The DC-10, like other aircraft, has "artificial feel" built into it, so that when things are automated and computerized, the pilot still gets the feel of an airplane, as opposed to just sitting there and operating a computer. For instance, when you accelerate, you need to put forward pressure and then "trim it out" almost like you would a sailboat.

Our training took on a round robin feel. While I was training up front as captain with an instructor in the right seat, Dale would be getting his flight engineer panel time. Then we'd switch. In that way I was able to keep the cost down—way down. The cost of the simulator was about one tenth that of a real airplane and we only got charged for the actual simulator time, so we were able to share the expense between us.

The deal with the FAA was that they would come give me my check ride in the real airplane as a flight engineer. Then I would switch to the front seat and take my check ride as the captain. If I failed, then they would require additional training *in the airplane*. That meant I had one chance to do it right. There was no way I could afford to fail and then rent the airplane for training at a cost of $4,000 per hour.

Check-ride day came, and I was breathless. By that time word had gotten out around the training center that a woman was taking a check ride for a DC-10 type rating. There were about sixteen people on board that DC-10 when we took off.

In addition to voyeurs, there was a technical manual writer who joined us named Tom Speer, an ex-Air Force colonel who was able to cut his own deal with United. He later became a line pilot for United, and did some of the DC-10 training videos for the company. I was to cross paths with Tom many times years later when we were both flying as pilots for United.

It was like a bizarre game of musical chairs. I sat at the panel and passed my flight engineer check ride, and then Dale sat down and passed his. In the meantime, a few of the flight managers were up front flying the airplane.

After I got my flight engineer rating I did something I had always wanted to do. With everyone up front in or just outside the cockpit, there was nobody to stop me and nobody was watching. I took off my shoes and, in my stocking feet, stood at the front of the airplane leaning forward like a ski jumper while the plane readied for takeoff. A DC-10 has an exceptionally high pitch on takeoff, and I thought it would be really fun to "ski" down the aisle, which is why I was now standing all the way forward, facing rearward in my stocking feet.

I shoved off on the next takeoff and got going so fast I thought I might hit the rear wall and go right through it. I had to catch myself about halfway down the coach cabin and start over to keep from getting out of control. Also, the friction was intense enough that the bottom of my feet burned, but it was really fun! Then I went up front. It was my turn to go act like an adult and to *be the captain.*

We started our flight late in the afternoon, around four-thirty or something like that. There were at least eight check rides that day with Dale, Tom, all those flight managers and me. There were so many I sort of lost count.

Although normally the copilot or PNF (pilot not flying) would do all the radio communications, the pilot in the right seat turned to me and said, "Meryl, you do the calls, okay?"

"Sure, but why?"

He smiled, and responded, "I just wonder if anyone's going to notice a lady flying a jumbo jet."

I smiled, too, and they did notice.

ATC radioed right away. "Is there a problem? What's the deal with the woman on the radio"?

The instructor pilot in the right seat, Jerry, said, "We've got the world's first DC-10 lady captain's rating ride in progress."

I knew what I was doing was unusual, but I actually hadn't considered things quite like that. I turned to the FAA check airman. "Is that really true?"

"Yep, so far as I know. Not only that, but you're almost certainly the youngest person to check out in this position anywhere in the world." All I could do was stare at him blankly. To this day I don't know if somewhere in the world a younger pilot had done this, or maybe even another woman, but there wasn't one anywhere in the United States and the FAA later said they were pretty certain it was true.

*Wow.* It startled me to think I might be the very first woman doing this or, at age twenty-seven, the youngest person. Doing what I was doing had nothing at all to do with being a woman. I just wanted to be an airline pilot. But it was still pretty amazing to me.

The instructor even had me make a PA (public address) announcement to the "passengers." I can't remember what I said, but I actually did imagine an airplane full of passengers, and it felt so good. Sadly, it was as close as I was going to get for a while.

It was Liberace at the Hollywood Bowl without an audience all over again, although I was not to hear that story until I'd actually started writing this book. First time around, Liberace played to a handful of people—the groundskeepers—in the Hollywood Bowl. I "played" to an "audience" of United staff in a DC-10.

Although things change with the times, at that time pilots would spend as many as eighteen years just as flight engineers before being able to upgrade even to the right seat, or copilot position. Everything was, and still is, based upon seniority, and movement was incredibly slow. In fact, during the very time period all this happened, United had actually hired its first few women pilots but they had already been laid off or were about to be. The first one, Gail Gorski, was hired in Januuary, 1978 and was featured on the cover of *Parade* magazine. The caption on the article inside read something like, "Female Pilots Get Their Turn". Another one of these very first women pilots at United was featured in at least one magazine ad for a credit card. Both are still with United today.

Even though it was for such a short time, I was thrilled that I was sitting in the captain's seat of an actual United Airlines DC-10. The timing was right, as far as being a woman, and I was determined to make it next time hiring began. That wasn't to happen for another six years or so, and even then I was hired in an especially turbulent time in United's history.

Everybody passed their check rides, I'm happy to say. And every person on that airplane, from my United instructor, Jerry Warnke, to the FAA inspector, said, "Congratulations, Captain Getline," after my own ride was complete. It was one of those special Life Moments you never forget.

When we got back to the training center, it was late—past midnight. Buddy thought we'd be gone just a couple of hours at most and had waited to be the first to (hopefully) congratulate me. When we didn't return until after midnight he was frantic with worry. He had no idea anyone was on board but Dale, me, Tom, the FAA inspector and my United flight instructor, Jerry.

"Where *were* you guys? I was just about ready to launch a search!" And he hugged and congratulated me. I couldn't believe he "waited up" for me. The section of the training center where his office was located was otherwise dark and completely deserted.

I was later to fly the DC-10 as a pilot for United Airlines, first as a flight engineer (second officer) and then as a copilot. United sold its passenger DC-10s before I was able to fly them from the left seat. I didn't take an opening for all-cargo flying. Some of the fun definitely goes out of it when it's all cargo, at least for me. Other pilots prefer not dealing with passengers, but to my mind they're missing out. It's why I wanted to be an airline pilot. I love flying and I love the idea of safely getting people where they need to go.

## CHAPTER 25

## Wing Walker

One day, while still flying with Inland Empire Airlines out of Fresno, one of my fellow captains, Darryl Silva, introduced me to his friend Bob Crouch, who was visiting from Alaska. Bob was a pilot for Arco, but had heard that a company called Wien (a family name, pronounced "Ween") Air Alaska was hiring. Their base was in Anchorage, they had just acquired some B-727's, and were about to hire.

I got an interview at Wien, where I expected not to have any difficulties being a female pilot. Wien actually had a female pilot already, Nancy Lane, who was well liked and respected as both a person and as a pilot, so I was expecting an easier time of it. I was wrong.

Airlines almost universally required a flight engineer's rating to get hired, but then they would provide training anyway. The fact that my engineer's rating was in the DC-10 intrigued them, but not as much as the type-rating. Even though Wien never expected to fly anything larger than the 727, the interviewer stated that he actually would not have hired another woman except for that rating. "If you can fly a DC-10, you can fly a 727." And with that, I was a Wien pilot.

Wien Air Alaska was my first real airline job, and needless to say, I was excited. I would be flying what I considered "real" planes for a regional carrier: 727's and 737's. The job at Wien allowed me to fly jets for the first time, other than the occasional Lear or other corporate jet. In 1981 I relocated to Anchorage. After some initial trepidation that I'd be furloughed before even making it to training, as had previously happened with TWA, Hughes Airwest and a few other companies, I got settled in quickly.

Wien Air Alaska was a family-owned company. Two of the Wien brothers were still flying at the time. Merrill and Bob, Sr., had been around for ages, as had some of my new colleagues. One older Wien pilot showed me his license, signed by Orville Wright. Bob Wien, Jr., was also a pilot, and he later went to fly for United after Wien Air Alaska went out of business.

Although we usually flew scheduled passenger flights, there were also cargo and charter flights, most commonly to the "North Slope" of Alaska. We'd fly workers back and forth from the oil camps where the people who maintained the Alaska Pipeline stayed for several weeks or months at a time.

Unbelievably, these sites were luxurious, self-contained communities complete with all the amenities any upscale neighborhood would have. There were movie theaters, shops, music halls with pianos I'd play every chance I got, soft ice cream and popcorn carts around every corner and gourmet food in the dining halls. British Petroleum even used their reservoir as a swimming pool.

There were only about two hundred pilots at Wien. I started out on reserve (on call) as a B-727 flight engineer. My very first flight happened to be on my twenty-eighth birthday in 1981. I assumed I was taking a regular passenger flight, but it turned out to be a photo mission. A Learjet was to fly alongside our B-727 as we flew formation with a Wien B-737 around Mt. McKinley, which tops out at 21,320 feet. Our altitude was only

17,000 feet, making for some dramatic shots. The company
gave each pilot who flew that day a commemorative photo of
the two Wien jets circling the mountain, and we were later to
see the pictures taken that day in various magazine ads.

Several Wien pilots went out of their way to make me feel
welcome, some ignored me, and others let me know I was not
wanted. "We don't need or want women in our cockpits," one
captain informed me during my first couple of weeks on the job.
"Why don't you just go back where you came from and stick to
Cessna-150's or, better yet, go home and have babies?" Lovely.

I flew for Wien, often laid off for months at a time, until it
finally folded. During one period of being laid off, when it
looked like the furlough was going to last awhile I called in to a
local radio program on Anchorage's 750 AM KFQD that helped
people who were out of work. I was an anomaly, not just a pilot,
but a woman pilot. The host, Herb Shaindlin, a local ABC TV
News commentator and radio talk-show host, invited me on a
two-hour radio show as his guest. The show was so well received
by both the call-in audience and Herb himself, that I was a guest
again just a couple of weeks later for a second two-hour show. I
had a lot of stories to tell, and Herb and I developed a close
friendship during the course of those appearances.

Herb was also well known for his radio and TV commercials for various local businesses. I had some ideas and, along
with Herb and his producer Fred Marx, created some new radio
spots for some local restaurants. It was surprising and gratifying
when I received a writer's award—"Best of the North"—for my
very first creative endeavor. I went on to help produce about a
half dozen more radio commercials, performing in some of
them. Herb was certainly used to it, but it was a novelty and a
kick to hear myself on the various commercials throughout the
day.

Herb was a New Yorker who'd come to Alaska decades ago for a short stay and never left. He was constantly moaning about the lack of good New York hot dogs—specifically Nathan's Hot Dogs—which at that time were available only on Times Square and Coney Island.

Finally I couldn't stand it anymore. One night I went to the airport, climbed aboard a Flying Tigers B-747, flew to New York's JFK Airport, got dropped off at Times Square by one of the flight crew, picked up a couple of cases of Nathan's Hot Dogs, took the "Carey Bus" back out to JFK and hopped a ride back to Anchorage, again courtesy of Flying Tigers.

I had tried to get Nathan's to arrange shipment for me, but I couldn't get them to cooperate. Certainly shipping them would have been more efficient, but I didn't know anyone at all in New York to handle it, so I just went and did it myself.

Herb was overwhelmed both at receiving his beloved hot dogs and at the fact that I would go to all that trouble. It was no big deal for me. A free trip to New York, a free trip back. The only thing I paid for was the hot dogs themselves and the bus ride out to JFK from Nathan's in Times Square. It made good fodder for his radio show, though.

It was through being on Herb's program that I was ultimately hired by the Nondalton Indian tribe to help them get their air taxi certificate. Because of the Native Claims Settlement Act, many of Alaska's Indian tribes had been awarded large sums of cash and now were looking for things to do with it. Since many areas of Alaska were (and are) remote, with no roads at all, the best means of transportation was by air. The Nondalton Indian tribe wanted their own air taxi and I was hired as their Chief Pilot to get their certification. Jim, the tribal chief, loved having a woman as his Chief Pilot. Scott Gustafson was a young pilot already working for them when I got there and has since become a United pilot. Scott and I became good friends and he'd take me flying in his Super Cub into the Alaskan back-country where we'd land on sandbars and in other remote areas.

The Alaskan wilderness by air is beautiful, and the fact that you can see so much by air made my flying time in Alaska among the most memorable. I must say, however, that it's always better to see the scenery from *inside* the plane.

Pilots generally carry their logbooks with them so they can log each flight as it happens. I still have my logs from every flight I ever took, as any pilot does. Flight logs are like academic tran-scripts or employment history. You simply cannot get a flying job without having logs to show what you've done. Naturally, then, pilots protect their logbooks like their own children.

One day I dropped off some of my Indian passengers at their settlement in Nondalton, located south of Anchorage and on the opposite side of the Cook Inlet, a finger of water maybe fifty miles wide leading to the Gulf of Alaska. I was on my way back to Anchorage, alone in the company Skymaster. Made by Cessna, this high-wing aircraft was sometimes called a "Mixmaster," referring to the push-pull propellers—one on the front and one on the back. There was a pressurized and unpres-surized version of the aircraft. Ours was pressurized.

I put the soft vinyl briefcase that held my current logbook and other papers on the seat next to me. Everything was fine until I reached ten thousand feet. I wasn't doing much, just fly-ing along, enjoying myself, when suddenly there was a major explosive sound, like a cannon being shot right there in the cockpit. My door, half of which opened upward, had suddenly blown open! When a balloon is pricked, you hear the pop as the air inside explodes outward. It's the same thing in an airplane: the air inside equalizes with the air outside, and everything wants to go out.

I was belted in, of course, but everything on the seat beside me went out, including the airplane flight manual and my briefcase with my logbook in it! The flight manual could be replaced, but *not the logbook!* Here was another instance where I thought, *There goes my airline career.* All of my flight time at Wien was in that book, with both B-727 and B-737 time, and hundreds of hours prior to that. You can't just tell an airline you lost it. That's the equivalent of "The dog ate my homework."

I groaned. At least, I think I did; I couldn't hear a thing except the horrific, deafening roar of the wind. The air equalized in just a moment or two, but the noise remained almost unbearable. I looked at my aircraft instruments, fearing my rear propeller might have suffered some damage from stuff being sucked out and then through it. But everything looked normal and the aircraft was flying fine.

A spot of color out of the corner of my eye caught my attention. My briefcase was wrapped around the strut of the airplane that ran from the body, at an angle, up to the wing. My logbook was right there, but just out of reach!

I thought it through. When I slowed the airplane down for landing, when I put out flaps or gear, would it stay wrapped around the strut or would it, at some point, fall off? I decided I'd been given a second chance and wasn't going to waste it. If it fell off, I would never forgive myself.

The aircraft had no autopilot, but the air was smooth and I trimmed up the airplane the best I could to keep it as level as possible. "Don't think about it—just do it!" I commanded myself. I crouched in the doorway of the airplane and reached out, but the briefcase was all the way at the end of the strut, which was slightly behind the door and at a steep angle up to the wing. There was no way I could even come close to reaching it. If I wanted my logbook back, I'd have to go out and get it. I was afraid if I turned, or slowed down, or absolutely anything else changed at all, it would drop off. There was no time to lose.

I started laying myself down along the strut, grabbing it with both hands, thumbs on top, fingers locked on the bottom side of the thin metal bar that was the strut. The strut was located slightly aft of the doorway and it was very awkward. To reach the briefcase, I had to stretch out almost the whole way, on my stomach, only my toes inside the airplane, hooked around the ledge of the doorframe. *Don't look down!* I screamed mentally. *Whatever you do, don't look down!* I looked down. *Big* mistake. Ten thousand feet below the icy water was churning with whitecaps. I refused to consider the possibility that I might fall off. The airplane would be left to crash, hopefully away from civilization somewhere—not hard to do in Alaska.

My fingers still locked, I was able to somehow drag the briefcase along the strut using my chin to help maneuver it toward me and the airplane, but keeping its relative position on the strut the same, letting the force of the wind keep it taut against the strut until we were both safely back inside the airplane. My altitude was almost where I'd left it, just a couple hundred feet high, course only a few degrees off.

I was close enough to Anchorage now that I radioed the tower directly. I had to do it "in the blind" meaning I was broadcasting but could not hear anything due to the incredible noise level inside my plane. I had already put in a transponder (radar) code to alert Anchorage to the fact that I was having an emergency. I wasn't sure what they could hear of what I said, if anything, but broadcast at intervals my situation, that I was headed in for landing but unable to hear any transmissions at all.

A control tower has a light gun for aircraft that have lost radio communications, and I saw the green light as I came in, signaling that the way had been cleared for me to come in and land. I had already broadcast that I'd had a door blow open and had requested emergency equipment standing by. I wasn't sure what to expect regarding aircraft performance with that great big door interfering with the aerodynamics of the airplane. At least it had stayed attached.

My senses were possibly somewhat dulled by the constant deafening noise, not to mention the fact that I was almost in shock regarding the excursion outside the plane, but it didn't seem that my airplane's performance was noticeably affected.

After I landed, the control tower told me they saw an explosion of white come out my rear propeller. The "explosion" turned out to be what we assumed later was the flight manual, reduced to a cloud of confetti. Upon landing it had loosened itself from wherever it had been hung up and finally gone through the rear propeller, which surprisingly was undamaged. At least the flight manual was replaceable.

A worried mechanic rushed up to my window. "What the hell happened?"

"Door wasn't latched properly."

He whistled. "Jeez."

"I know," I said, far more calmly than I actually felt. "I hate it when that happens."

## CHAPTER 26

# At Last

Eventually, I was called back from being furloughed at Wien. I had accomplished the mission with the Nondalton tribe, getting them their air taxi certificate for Raven Air, as they called their small airline.

Wien ultimately failed, though, and I was laid off—for good this time. The majors were now much more open to employing women, and I heard United was once again hiring. I was finally brought on board by United on May 29, 1985.

Of course, though my years-long dream of being hired by United, of being employed by one of the majors, was now realized, it wasn't complete. Just before I was hired, United pilots went on strike. Not only was my job in jeopardy, but so also was my entire career as a United pilot. As with all the other events in my life, this turned out to be something of a detour itself. It was especially difficult to experience any more obstacles when I was finally so close to donning the United uniform. For a while it looked as if I might never actually fulfill my dream. Although the strike certainly caused some major difficulties, I did manage to hang on.

I had a terrific time working my way up to the left seat, the captain's position, which I finally attained on November 24th, 1991. I spent a number of years flying from San Francisco to

Hawaii, a classic United route that had helped the Islands gain statehood. I flew everything from "regular" passengers to chartered Super Bowl flights for the teams (yes, it *is* more fun flying the winners!) and loads of celebrities and politicians—even a baby Pygmy hippo was aboard one flight. I was stationed in New Zealand for a short time during the Persian Gulf War when many of United's planes were requisitioned for military charter, causing a shortage of aircraft in the South Pacific.

Another time, I flew one of United's very first flights to Tokyo, and got to fly to Bangkok, Singapore, Hong Kong and other points in the Far East when United first acquired those routes from Pan American.

In the early years, when I was unattached and free to travel wherever and whenever I was called, I would sometimes be gone for a couple of weeks at a time. On one trip to Maui, I was getting ready to turn around and head back to San Francisco when I got a call to go to Honolulu to commence a two-week trip to the Far East. The assigned copilot had broken his leg while in Honolulu. Another one would be flown out to replace me for my trip from Maui back to San Francisco.

It was then that I'd realized I packed for a day trip, not a whole two weeks. There's a pilot's version of Murphy's Law that states: the one time you don't pack a complete suitcase, you'll get called on to fly a days-long trip. Such was the case for me. I called United back and they told me to go shopping in Honolulu and expense everything. My trip wouldn't leave until the next day so I had plenty of time. You gotta love this job!

One of the great things about flying—aside from the flying itself—is the opportunity to travel all over the world and take people places they need and want to go. Also involved is the interaction with the passengers that I just love. United, unlike any other airline, holds a channel open to allow our passengers to hear communications between the cockpit and air traffic control. It's an optional feature for the pilots to use and many of us do use it. It's a very popular feature with many of our passengers.

I enjoy speaking with my passengers and still (even since 9/11) welcome passengers into my cockpit before and after each flight whenever possible. I also continue to speak to folks mainly via the PA (public address) system; it's a wonderful way to let passengers in on what's happening. It can be something as simple as pointing out an interesting landmark, or explaining something they may have heard on Channel 9.

For example, I had a recent flight which was designated "Lifeguard 268" for communications purposes with air traffic control. I knew what it was, but suspected most people did not, so I got on the PA and explained that we were carrying an organ on its way to a recipient. Many people don't realize that airlines often carry organs cross-country for emergency recipients, so I explained this to my passengers. "Incidentally," I added, "This is a lunch flight. I'd stay away from the liver." I could hear them laughing through the cockpit door.

I've continued to love flying at night, although I've long since gotten over the airsickness associated with daytime travel. There is nothing more beautiful than gliding along in the clear night sky toward a new dawn, or skimming on top of a cloud layer with a bright moon above, the reflection off the clouds below all soft and silver.

Pilots witness sights every day that people with ground jobs may never see at all: the sun of a new day peeking above the curve of the Earth, or a "red eclipse," which happens when an eclipse of the moon coincides with the setting sun. I never get tired of seeing the otherworldly glow of the Northern Lights, or meteor showers, or giant electrical storms, or the Milky Way on a moonless night. There is no end to the sense of awe I feel even after more than thirty years as a pilot.

I was almost thirty-two years old when I was finally hired at United Airlines. It was almost too late for me; just a short time prior, I would have been too old to get hired. The age cut-off for every airline I was aware of was thirty-one-and-a-half until one of the airlines got sued for age discrimination and lost. That was the end of the age barrier.

I am now fifty years old; over half of my flying career has been with United Airlines. And you know what? I still love what I do: from that very first flight when I was eleven years old and got so airsick, all the way up to and including today—I love to fly.

Age sixty and mandatory retirement aren't that far away for me now, and I dread my last flight for United Airlines. I can always continue to fly planes privately as long as my health holds out, but it won't be the same. It's not just the act of flying itself— it's being the guardian for a planeload of passengers—the responsibility of getting everyone where they're going safely.

Had I come along just a few years later than I did, things would have been very different, but much less colorful. Many more doors would have been opened for women by that time. It would have been a given that women could fly, and there were flight schools opening up all over. Although it can cost a near fortune to attend aviation schools, they have cropped up all over the country, offering training to men and women alike.

Still, I'm glad that I started when I did. Had I not done so, my story would be quite different, and frankly, I like it just fine the way it is. There are certain things I would not have wanted to miss, and certain events I could have done without. But right now, as I gaze out the window and fly toward another breath-taking sunset, I wouldn't change a thing.

## AFTERWORD

For as long as I can remember, my Mom has "bugged" me to write a book based on my life's adventures. I honestly thought this was because she was my mother and not because I had anything particularly interesting to say. It was only after listening to some twenty-year-old radio interviews I did on a local talk-show while living in Anchorage, Alaska, that I realized I actually have had a more-interesting-than-average life. Listening to those interviews after so long not only made me laugh—they made me think that maybe my story actually could be of some use to others who might be discouraged by where they are in life.

On one of my recent United flights, my First Officer, John Fry, suggested that I'm the sort of person who never takes "no" for an answer. As I thought about his comment I realized that this is true. It's made the difference between getting what I wanted instead of taking what I was offered. Simple as this revelation was, I know first hand it's not always easy pursuing our goals. The difficulty seems to lie in MAKING THE DECISION to be assertive rather than BEING assertive. Fortunately for me, I seem to have been born with assertiveness built in. But for those born without it, it truly is necessary to acquire it or risk stagnating in an empty, unfulfilling life, and what a terrible waste that would be.

For those who ask how I've gotten where I am, my response is that I knew from an early age exactly what I wanted, and wouldn't let anything derail me from achieving my goals. If you are unsure of your goals, then your first priority should be to decide what they are, then don't just hope they happen—MAKE them happen.

It was impossible to include in this book all of the many adventures which happened in the pursuit of my dream to be an airline captain for United Airlines, but I'm hoping my readers will be entertained and maybe even a little inspired to pursue the infinite possibilities available to each and every one of us.

As the saying goes, "It's not what happens to us that matters—it's what we do about it." I've made this my own life's motto. It's more fun than letting Life beat us to death.

> Meryl Getline
> Summer 2004
> Elizabeth, CO

## FAQ'S

### Get Your Aviation Questions Answered!

Do you have some questions about aviation? Want to know what a certain term means? Have you ever wondered how runways are designated? Do you ever look out the window during a plane ride and ask yourself, 'What are those things on the end of the wings for?' Want to know how certain weather affects aircraft or how it's determined which pilots fly which airplanes and on what routes? Did you ever wonder how we pilots can land at any airport and find our way around on the ground?

You get the idea! If you have a question you'd like to ask an airline pilot, or if you'd like to make a comment, then simply subscribe to my FREE online newsletter called *From The Cockpit*. Get your own questions answered, or simply read what others are asking.

To subscribe, log onto **www.fromthecockpit.com** and click on Free Newsletter.

**OR**

Simply let me know you wish to subscribe by writing to me directly at info@fromthecockpit.com and I'll take care of it for you!

Your contact information will NOT be shared with anyone else and you may unsubscribe at any time.

## Sample Questions & Answers
## From Online Newsletter FromTheCockpit

*Where did you learn to fly, and how did you wind up with*
*United Airlines? Did you come up through the military?*

This is by FAR the question I am most often asked. Hence the
book *The World At My Feet*. Please turn to page one and START
READING!

*What is the most technically difficult airport you fly into and*
*why?*

Of course this answer will vary depending upon which pilot is
asked. For me, I would have to say Mexico City would be my
Number One pick. It's at a relatively high altitude, over 7,000
feet, which reduces airplane performance somewhat because of
the thinner air. All U.S. airports we fly into, at least that I am
aware of (with the exception of Jackson Hole, Wyoming which
uses a different runway surface to help with moisture) have
"grooved" runways, allowing rainwater to drain off. Mexico
City's runways are very long but ungrooved. Even the smallest
amount of rain makes them slippery. Also, the most common
approach into Mexico City, landing in a northeasterly direction,
requires a sharp turn onto final very close to the landing, which
is just a little awkward as a steeper bank than normal is
required. Communications aren't great there, either. Although
English is required internationally, sometimes the Mexican controllers are difficult to understand. Just all part of the fun!

*What's your favorite airplane?*

I don't want to sound as if I'm dodging the question, but the
honest truth, echoed by many pilots I've asked the same

question, is "Whatever airplane I'm flying." There has never been an airplane I've flown that I've disliked. Whatever I'm flying at the moment is my favorite. Right now it's the Airbus, both A-319 and A-320. The Airbus is the only aircraft operated by United that utilizes a "sidestick" as opposed to the more traditional control column to steer the airplane.

The stick is not like the stick in some military and older domestic planes, which directly controlled the aircraft. Our sidestick, by comparison, inputs signals, which are then responded to by the aircraft's computers. It takes very gentle inputs. Most pilots enjoy the sidestick because it gives us a lot more space in the cockpit. Also, there's a little tray table that folds out. No more meals in our laps. You gotta love that!

### How do pilots navigate around airports on the ground? Aren't some airports pretty complicated?

Yes, some airports are VERY complicated, like Chicago O'Hare. Pilots are issued "plates" (charts) not only for aerial navigation, but also for ground navigation. We have charts which show the names of all the runways, taxiways, terminals, etc. The physical runways, taxiways, terminals, etc. have markings on them. It's pretty much like reading a street map.

### How do guys feel about women in the cockpit?

These days it is thankfully pretty much a non-issue. Most of my copilots are quite a bit younger than I am, and they are more used to women in positions of authority. Previously, however, it was quite a different story. There was a time, not so long ago, when many men were extremely hostile toward women in the cockpit. Being a captain makes a difference, and the changing attitudes toward women in general in our society has made a difference as well. These days, as a general statement, I'd say most guys are okay with it, and if they're not, they hide their feelings better than they used to!

### Do the airlines use navigators?

Nope, not necessary. We know the way. (Just KIDDING!) Modern aircraft are equipped with everything we pilots need to navigate ourselves. Gone are the days when navigators were required.

### Do you get to choose where you fly? What routes do you generally fly?

Everything we do as pilots is based on seniority. Each month, each aircraft type has published "lines" of flying, and we "bid" for what we want based upon our seniority. It's complicated, and there are computer programs to help us, one written by my good friend and United Captain Scott Gustafson, with whom I flew in Alaska (see Chapter 25 of The World At My Feet). Then, we can trade trips around if we still don't like what we got. No matter what we get—even our first choice—the minute the monthly lines are "awarded" it's a mad scramble for some of us to rearrange everything as fast and as much as possible. This certainly doesn't go for everyone, but I know many of us have outside interests and it's always a challenge to coordinate our schedules accordingly. So the answer is, it depends upon our seniority and the trip sequences that United develops for us each month—a daunting task for our scheduling department, by the way. I'd say that I'm generally satisfied with my schedules each month, but that's because of my seniority with relation to the aircraft I fly. When I was more junior, I pretty much flew what was left over, which may not have always suited my personal wants.

### *Do you fly more than one airplane?*

United's policy is that we train for one airplane at a time and then fly only that airplane. When our seniority allows it, if we change aircraft, then it's back to school at our training center in Denver where we go through ground school, simulator training, and then go out on the line with passengers and a check airman. I'd say total time from the first day of school to the last is around six weeks or so, give or take a couple of weeks depending upon scheduling. One airplane may include two models. For instance, we Airbus pilots fly both the A-320 and A-319. It's basically the same aircraft although there are some minor differences, and the A-320 is slightly larger. Pilots on the B-767, a wide-body, also fly the B-757, a narrow-body aircraft. But the answer is basically we do not mix aircraft—just flying one type before moving on to the next.

### *What's your favorite layover?*

Obviously, this refers to a personal preference. My answer is— anywhere involving a beach. I'd put Hawaii first. I flew there while on the DC-10 but the Airbus doesn't go there, so I haven't been out to the Islands for awhile. On the routes I fly now, San Juan, Puerto Rico, Miami and Ft. Lauderdale are my favorites. For city layovers, it's San Francisco, Seattle and New York. Why? Respectively, lots of sightseeing, pretty scenery, good food.

### *Do you ever get tired of your job?*

No.

To Order Additional Copies of *The World At My Feet* call 1-800-345-6665 or log onto www.fromthecockpit.com and click on "The Book!"